GW01606239

The Dorling Kindersley

ILLUSTRATED FAMILY ENCYCLOPEDIA

VOLUME 5 CONTENTS, CYCLING – EUROPE, CENTRAL

LONDON, NEW YORK, MUNICH,
MELBOURNE AND DELHI

Senior Editor Jayne Parsons

Senior Art Editor Gillian Shaw

Project Editors
Marian Broderick, Gill Cooling, Maggie Crowley, Hazel Egerton, Cynthia O'Neill, Veronica Pennycook, Louise Pritchard, Steve Setford, Jackie Wilson

Project Art Editors
Jane Felstead, Martyn Foote, Neville Graham, Jamie Hanson, Christopher Howson, Jill Plank, Floyd Sayers, Jane Tetzlaff, Ann Thompson

Editors
Rachel Beaugié, Nic Kynaston, Sarah Levete, Karen O'Brien, Linda Sonntag

Art Editors
Tina Borg, Diane Clouting, Tory Gordon-Harris

DTP Designers
Andrew O'Brien, Cordelia Springer

Managing Editor Ann Kramer

Managing Art Editor Peter Bailey

Senior DTP Designer Mathew Birch

Picture Research Jo Walton, Kate Duncan, Liz Moore

DK Picture Library Ola Rudowska, Melanie Simmonds

Country pages by PAGE*One*: Bob Gordon, Helen Parker, Thomas Keenes, Sarah Watson, Chris Clark

Cartographers Peter Winfield, James Anderson

Research Robert Graham, Angela Koo

Editorial Assistants Sarah-Louise Reed, Nichola Roberts

Production Louise Barratt, Charlotte Traill

First published in Great Britain in 1997, 2004
by Dorling Kindersley Limited,
80 Strand, London WC2R 0RL

This edition published in 2004 by MDS BOOKS/MEDIASAT Group in association with MediaFund Limited

www.mediasatgroup.com

A CIP catalogue record for this book is available from the British Library

ISBN: 84 9789 537 1 (ISBN of the collection)
ISBN: 84 9789 525 8 (ISBN of this volume)
ISSN: 1744 2214

Not to be sold separately from the Daily Mail

Colour reproduction by Colourscan, Singapore
Printed and bound in the E.U.

CYCLING

CYCLE SPORTS are held on tracks, roads, and cross-country circuits. Races range from 1,000-m (1,094-yd) sprints on an indoor track to multi-stage events over hundreds of kilometres that last a week or more. Special courses are prepared for off-road racing, which includes cyclocross and mountain-bike racing. Racers ride specialized bikes for the different races. Some need to be be as light as possible; others need to be strong, and the top riders have bicycles made for them to their own specifications.

Track racing

Track races take place on wooden indoor tracks, with banked sides, or flat asphalt outdoor tracks. Races include sprints, in which riders jockey for position before making a last-lap dash, and pursuits, in which riders start on opposite sides of the track, the race won by the fastest rider or when one catches the other.

Riders crouch over the handlebars in a streamlined position.

Disc wheels are more efficient indoors because there is no cross-wind.

Track bicycles have no gears or brakes.

Pursuit bicycle

Saddle is set high for more pedalling power.

Criterium bicycle

Composite wheel

Spoked wheel

British cyclist Chris Boardman on his revolutionary Lotus bike

Types of wheel

The design and material of wheels are constantly being improved to suit particular uses. Weight and shape are the important factors. Using spokes saves weight, but increases drag.

Team pursuit

In team pursuit, riders take turns to lead their group of four. The time of the third rider in each team determines the result. One rider usually makes an all-out effort near the finish before trailing off.

Time-trials

In time-trials, competitors ride as fast as possible, on their own, over a set distance or for a fixed time. Time-trials are some of the hardest races and require continuous effort.

Road racing

Races take place on courses set along ordinary roads. There are single-stage races and multi-stage events such as the Tour de France, in which the total time determines placings. In individual and team time-trials on the road, the riders start at intervals. Criterium races are 40–100 km (25–62 miles) long. They take place over short courses with many laps, along city streets and through parks.

Tour de France

The world's leading road race is the Tour de France which lasts about three weeks. The overall leader on total time wears the famous yellow jersey for the next stage.

Miguel Indurain

Spanish road racer Miguel Indurain (b. 1964) became the first cyclist to win the Tour de France in five successive years (1991–95), equalling the record number of wins. In 1996, he took first place in the Olympic road time trial.

Off-road racing

Bicycles for off-road races have chunky tyres for the rough terrain. Cyclocross is the original form of cross-country cycling, with world championships since 1950. Mountain biking is now the most popular form, with world championships since 1990 and Olympic recognition in 1996.

Cyclocross

In cyclocross, races take place over laps of a cross-country course. Riders often find it quicker to dismount and carry their bikes over obstacles such as fences, gates, and ditches, and may have to run up steep hills or wade through water with them.

Mountain biking

Mountain bikes are built to survive rough handling. Most have steel-alloy frames, straight handlebars, and flat knobbly tyres. Courses for races have many climbs and descents, with routes over fields and gravel pits.

For log hopping, the rider must learn to shift her weight.

Weight over the rear wheel

Rider brings her weight over the front wheel.

Weight is kept over the front wheel until the hop has been completed.

FIND OUT MORE
BICYCLES AND MOTORCYCLES
FRANCE
HEALTH AND FITNESS
MOTOR SPORTS
OLYMPIC GAMES
SPORT

D

DAMS

IN MANY AREAS of the world, people rely on dams for their water and electricity supplies. A dam is a barrier that holds back water. The dam itself and the surrounding hills form a bowl in which water collects to form an artificial lake called a reservoir. Most dams are built across a river valley to catch the river's flow, but some dams create reservoirs into which water is pumped for storage. How strong a dam needs to be depends on the depth of the water in the reservoir. Some dams are enormous: the Grand Coulee Dam in the USA weighs nearly 10 million tonnes.

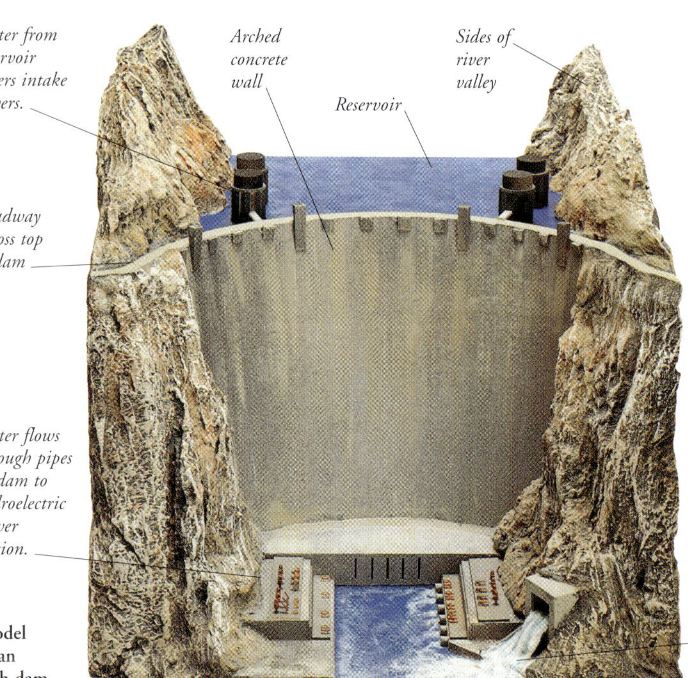

Model of an arch dam

Types of dam

There are three main types of dam: arch dams, gravity dams, and buttress dams. The type of dam that engineers decide to build depends on the geography of the location. Factors affecting the decision include the width and depth of the river valley and the type of rock around the site.

Buttress dam
A buttress dam is a huge concrete wall that leans into a reservoir of water. The wall is made up of concrete slabs that are supported on the downstream side of the dam by concrete projections known as buttresses.

Arch dam
An arch dam is built across the entrance to a narrow valley, so that the height of the dam is greater than its width. The dam's curved shape holds back water because it transfers the push of the water to the rock of the valley sides.

Gravity dam
A gravity dam is a huge embankment of earth or rock. Leakage is prevented by a waterproof clay core or a concrete skin on the upstream side of the dam. The dam's immense weight prevents the water from pushing it over.

Anatomy of a dam

This model shows an arch dam that creates a reservoir for supplying water and electricity to nearby towns and cities. The dam is made of thin concrete strengthened by thousands of steel bars. Water flowing through pipes in the dam drives electricity generators in the hydroelectric power station at the foot of the dam.

Flood control

On large rivers, dams help prevent flooding by holding back surges of flood water and releasing them downstream slowly. A flood barrier is a movable dam built across a tidal river. The barrier has gates that are usually open to allow the river to flow freely, but which can be closed when dangerously high tides threaten to surge upstream.

Model of Thames Flood Barrier, UK

Environmental effects

A river dam and the reservoir it forms can harm the environment. Huge areas of countryside are drowned by the reservoir, and the dam disrupts the river's natural flow, affecting wildlife and irrigation downstream. A dam also prevents fish from moving freely up and down the river.

Tidal barrage

A barrage is a dam across a river estuary that generates hydroelectric power. The dam holds back the tide as it ebbs and flows. The water is forced through pipes inside the barrage, where it drives electricity generators.

La Rance barrage, France

Weir

A weir is a low river dam that controls the flow of water by creating a stretch of deeper water upstream. Deep water makes the river navigable for boats.

Weir in Middlesex, England

FIND OUT MORE
BUILDING AND CONSTRUCTION | ELECTRICITY | ENERGY | FARMING | LAKES | OCEANS AND SEAS | RAIN | RIVERS | ROADS

DANCE

WHEN PEOPLE MOVE in time to music they are dancing. People have a natural urge to move in time to rhythms. Children jump up and down when they are excited; babies move naturally to rhythms they hear or feel. In dancing, these natural movements are organized into rhythmic and visual patterns. Different dances have developed all over the world, and are performed for different reasons. Dancing can be both an art form and recreation. It can express an emotion, tell a story, or set a mood.

Origins

Dancing is one of the oldest art forms. The first dances may have evolved from spontaneous stamping steps. These steps were later given rhythms and shapes and accompanied by grunts and shouts.

Australian Aboriginals performing the corroboree

Ceremonial dance
Early people found that rhythmic movements had a strong effect on the mind, and felt that dancing must have magical powers. They began to dance to ward off evil spirits, heal people, and ensure good crops.

Dance as entertainment
The ancient Egyptians were the first people known to use dancing simply as a form of entertainment. Professional dancing girls entertained the pharaoh and his guests at banquets, performing dances that included running, high kicks, and sensual hip movements.

Ancient Egyptian dancing girls

Chorus depicted on a Greek vase

Dance as theatre
The ancient Greeks made dance the basis of all their theatre. The chorus in a Greek play was a group of actors who danced and sang a commentary on the action.

Maasai dancers
The Maasai of East Africa move in straight lines as they dance, and include high jumps in their routines. As happens in all African dance, they are accompanied by rhythmic, exhilarating drumbeats.

African dance

Dancing is an essential part of life to many Africans, and important events, such as births, deaths, and initiation to adulthood, are all observed by dancing. African dances can last for many hours. The dances for men are usually very energetic, and include a lot of stamping and leaping. Women tend to do more gentle dances, clapping and swaying to the music or rhythm.

Asian dancing

The main influence on dance styles in Asia comes from India. Many Asian dances make use of stylized hand movements, particularly those from countries such as India, Sri Lanka, Burma, Thailand, and Cambodia.

Bent-back fingers

Head-dress

Indian dances
Indian classical dancers mime out stories from Indian mythology, and include sequences of more abstract dance movements.

There are six styles of Indian classical dance.

Dragon
The mythical dragon is a very important symbol in Chinese culture. Dragon dances are performed to celebrate festivals such as the Chinese New Year.

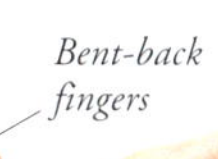

Dancers wear a dragon costume.

Southeast Asian dances
Classical dance in Southeast Asia typically includes slow, controlled movements, with many graceful hand and arm gestures. Dance-dramas, performed by highly trained dancers, are particularly popular in Indonesia and Thailand. Throughout the region there is a wide variety of traditional folk dances.

Royal Thai classical dancer

European folk dancing

Every European country has its folk dances, which are now essentially social. Some of them have been taken to other countries by settlers. The dances are often performed in traditional costumes, and many of them involve people forming simple patterns, such as lines and circles.

Flamenco
Perhaps the most famous of all Spanish dances is the flamenco. This dance is a mixture of both the Spanish and Arab cultures. The men use complicated footwork, while the women weave patterns with their arms. The dancers are accompanied by fast, dramatic guitar music.

Flamenco dancers also use their voices.

Irish dancing
Irish jigs are usually performed either by pairs or by individuals, but large groups also perform Irish dances. The jig is based on simple steps, but the dancers can elaborate and perform complicated leaping steps. They hold their upper body still and their arms straight down at their sides or holding hands. The dances are usually accompanied by the fiddle or bagpipes.

South American dancing

The dances of Central and South America reflect the cultures not only of the native peoples who have long occupied the region, but also of the European colonists and their African slaves. Many dances that originated in this region, such as the tango and samba, have become popular all over the world.

Macumba

The Macumba dance was taken to Brazil by African slaves as a form of voodoo-worship in which the dancer is believed to be possessed by a god. Macumba dancers worship Yemannjah, a goddess of the sea. Like all voodoo dances it involves shaking of the head and shoulders.

Tango

This dance originated in Argentina about 200 years ago. It had to be "cleaned up" before it became fashionable in Europe in the 1900s, because it was considered too immodest for the dance halls.

Contemporary dance

This style has no fixed technique. Dancers express their feelings in their movements. Contemporary dance began at the start of the 20th century, when US dancer Isadora Duncan broke away from ballet and developed her own style.

Samba

The samba was first danced in Brazil, especially at Carnival time, and became extremely popular in the United States and Europe in the early 1940s. It is danced by couples who perform simple backward and forward steps, swaying their bodies. In Brazil, there are many versions of the dance, each with a different rhythm, tempo, and mood.

Dancers adopt a flirtatious carnival mood.

There is no body contact in the samba.

A tilting pelvic action is required in many figures.

Dancers compete in the Rio de Janeiro Carnival every February.

Couples progress in an anti-clockwise direction.

Dancing the samba

Ballroom dancing

Developed in the courts of Europe, many ballroom dances, such as the waltz and samba, were adapted from folk dances. They were danced on flat, polished floors, which allowed for elegant gliding movements, rather than the jumping and stamping which folk dancers developed to cope with the rough floors or grass on which they danced.

Dancing the waltz

In competitions, dancers dress formally.

Partners dance in close contact with each other.

The couple progress around the dance floor in an anticlockwise direction.

Waltz

When the waltz first became popular with the aristocracy, in the 1700s, it caused a scandal because the couple was expected to dance close together. It was originally a simple Austrian peasant dance, but by the 19th century it was highly fashionable and composers such as Austrian Johann Strauss the younger (1825–99) specialized in writing waltz music.

Top-class dancers require strong ankles and a fit body.

Gene Kelly

American dancer Gene Kelly (1912–96) made film musicals popular with his athletic dance style. His best known films include *For Me and My Gal* (1942), *An American in Paris* (1951), and *Singin' in the Rain* (1952).

US dancer and actor Fred Astaire

Tap dance

In 19th-century America, black slaves combined African rhythms with the jigs of English and Irish settlers. Tap dance was thus created and became very popular.

Jazz dance

When jazz music became popular in the 1920s, an energetic, expressive form of dance developed with it. Today, jazz dancing is the main form of dancing in musicals and films.

Disco

Disco dancing became popular in the 1970s. The name comes from the clubs called discotheques, in which records were played for dancing. Couples usually dance facing, but not touching, each other, using simple repetitive movements.

FIND OUT MORE
BALLET · DRAMA · FILMS AND FILM-MAKING · JAZZ · MUSIC · OPERA · ROCK AND POP

DARWIN, CHARLES

THE BRITISH NATURALIST Charles Darwin is best known as the man who developed the remarkable theory of evolution by natural selection. The theory, which describes how one species can develop or evolve into another, caused a revolution in biological science. Darwin was not the first person to suggest a theory of evolution, but was the first to present a solid body of evidence for the idea. He also wrote books about his travels, coral reefs, barnacles, the pollination of flowers, and insect-eating plants.

Early life

Darwin was born in 1809, in Shrewsbury, England. His grandfather, Erasmus Darwin, had put forward his own theory of evolution in the 1790s. At first, Charles Darwin did not believe in the idea of evolution. He trained as a priest before studying geology and biology.

Galápagos Islands

Darwin studied thousands of plants and animals all around the world on the *Beagle*'s journey. The most interesting part was the few weeks spent in the Galápagos Islands, about 1,000 km (600 miles) from the coast of South America. Darwin noticed that the species there were different from those elsewhere in the world.

Notebooks used by Darwin in Galápagos Islands

List of species

Map pasted into notebook

Galápagos Islands

Notebooks

During his voyage on the *Beagle*, Darwin made careful, copious notes of everything he saw, gaining him the nickname "the old philosopher" from the ship's officers. The wealth of information he gathered helped him later, when he was developing his theory of evolution.

Darwin's finches

When he got home, Darwin realized that the finches on the Galápagos Islands had different beaks, depending on which island they inhabited. He decided that the birds had developed beaks that were best suited to the diet on their particular island.

The Beagle

At Cambridge, Darwin made friends with John Henslow, the professor of botany. Henslow suggested that Darwin would be a good choice as official naturalist on the naval survey ship HMS *Beagle*, which was about to sail around the world on a five-year scientific cruise. The trip lasted from 1831 to 1836.

Darwin's telescope

Darwin's watch

Fossil finds

When he landed in South America, Darwin found fossils of extinct animals, such as the giant sloth (now called *Mylodon darwini*), that closely resembled modern species. This suggested that animals had gradually changed to suit their environments.

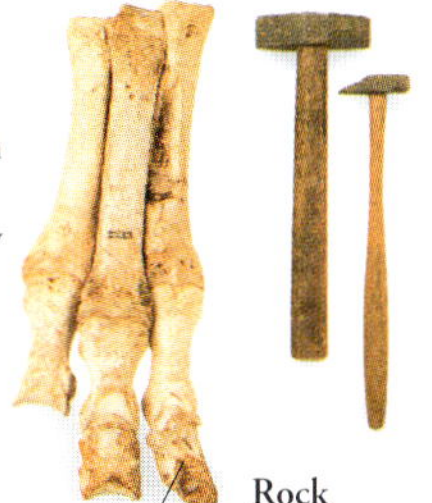

Bones of Macrauchenia, *a prehistoric mammal found by Darwin*

Rock hammers

The Origin of Species

Darwin returned to England and wrote an account of his travels. He spent years studying the specimens he had collected and the notes he had made. Gradually, he developed his idea that species evolved as animals adapted to suit their environments. He published his findings in his book *On the Origin of Species by Means of Natural Selection*. The work caused an outcry among Christians because it challenged the creation story in the Bible.

The naturalist

After his voyage, Darwin spent the rest of his life studying specimens, doing experiments, and writing up his findings. He never left England again, and for much of the rest of his life he was too ill to leave his home. Illness did not stop him working on subjects ranging from earthworms to the pollination of plants.

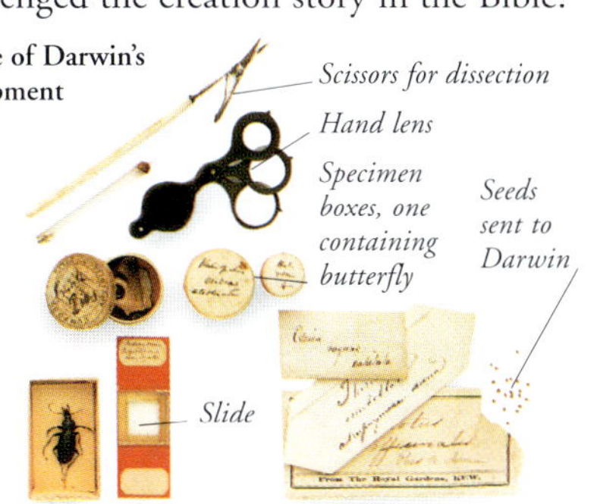

Some of Darwin's equipment

Scissors for dissection

Hand lens

Specimen boxes, one containing butterfly

Seeds sent to Darwin

Slide

Wallace

The British naturalist Alfred Russel Wallace (1823–1913) drew up a theory of evolution by natural selection quite independently of Darwin. He wrote to Darwin for advice, and the men wrote a paper about evolution together.

Natural selection

Parents produce many offspring, all different from each other. Only those best suited to their environment will survive, passing on some of their features to their offspring.

Lesser black-backed gull

Herring gull has same ancestor as Lesser black-backed, but has evolved separately.

CHARLES DARWIN

- 1809 Born in Shrewsbury, England.
- 1831 Sets sail on the *Beagle*.
- 1836 Returns to England.
- 1858 Wallace writes to Darwin about his evolutionary theory; they produce a paper on evolution together.
- 1859 Darwin publishes his *Origin of Species*.
- 1871 Publishes *The Descent of Man*, on human evolution.
- 1875 Publishes *Insectivorous Plants*, which describes how the sundew traps insects.
- 1880 Publishes *The Power of Movement in Plants*, which shows how light influences the direction of plant growth.
- 1882 Dies at Downe, England.

FIND OUT MORE
BIOLOGY · DINOSAURS · EVOLUTION · EXPLORATION · FOSSILS · GEOLOGY · HUMAN EVOLUTION · SCIENCE, HISTORY OF

DEER AND ANTELOPES

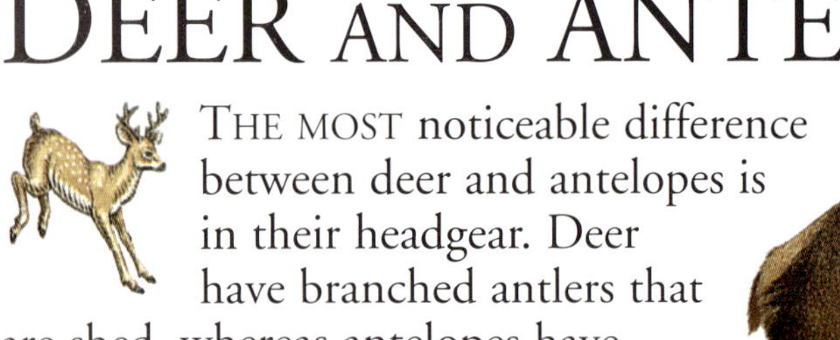

THE MOST noticeable difference between deer and antelopes is in their headgear. Deer have branched antlers that are shed, whereas antelopes have unbranched horns that are permanent. Both deer and antelopes are herbivorous hoofed mammals. They look similar to each other, but belong to different families. Deer are in a family of their own, while antelopes belong to the cattle family. They include gazelles, duikers, and spiral-horned antelopes.

Female red deer have no antlers.

Red deer
This is the most widespread deer. It is found across Europe and Asia, and as far as Japan, the Himalayas, and Australia.

Fringe-eared oryx
Oryx live in the arid grasslands of Tanzania and Kenya, in Africa. They obtain water from roots and tubers.

Both sexes have long, straight horns.

Stages of antler growth in a fallow deer

Antlers

The larger a stag's antlers, the more females it will attract. While the antlers are growing, they are protected by a velvety skin, richly supplied with blood vessels and nerves. At the end of the deer's breeding season, the blood supply to the antlers is cut off, causing the velvet to dry out and peel off in strips.

Deer

There are 38 species of deer spread over most of Europe, as well as Asia, North Africa, and the Americas. Some have been introduced into Australasia. Most species live in herds that split up in the breeding season. Most male deer, or stags, bear multi-branched antlers, which are shed and regrown every year.

Antelopes

Most of the 60 species of antelope live in Africa. Some, such as the blackbuck and the Tibetan antelope, are Asian. A few species have been introduced to other countries. Antelopes range in size from the giant Derby eland to the pygmy and royal antelopes, which are no bigger than hares.

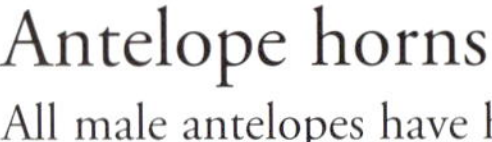

Antelope horns

All male antelopes have horns, but only some females. The males use their horns to intimidate their rivals and to defend their territory.

Horns are hollow.

Front view of hartebeest horns

Front view of greater kudu horns

Four-horned antelope
Males have two pairs of horns, making the deer a sought-after trophy for hunters. The front pair of horns is smaller than the back pair.

Nyala
The nyala, found in southeast African forests, has dark brown horns with a white tip. These can be up to 78 cm (31 in) long, with usually one open curve.

Hartebeest
Both male and female hartebeests have curved horns. Each has about 12 ridges but a smooth tip. Seen from the front, the horns are angular.

Greater kudu
The triple-spiralled horns of the male greater kudu are among the most imposing horns of any living animal. They grow up to 1.5 m (5 ft) long.

Roan antelope
Males and females have horns. About 55 cm (22 in) long, they are strongly ridged and curve gradually backward.

Browsing antelope

Grazing gazelles

Browsers and grazers
The antelopes include both grazing and browsing species. In Africa, for example, some species, such as Thomson's gazelle, graze on grass. Other species, such as the gerenuk, browse the leaves and shoots of trees. Grant's and dorcas gazelles browse and graze, according to what is available.

Largest and smallest deer

The largest of all deer is the moose of North America, known as the elk in Europe. An adult male moose may stand 1.8 m (6 ft) at the shoulder and weigh 545 kg (1,200 lbs). The smallest deer is the South American pudu, which stands only about 40 cm (16 in) at the shoulder and weighs about 9 kg (20 lbs).

Père David's deer
This deer once lived wild in China. Then, for 3,000 years, it existed only in parks. In 1865, the missionary Père David saw the last surviving herd. This herd was later wiped out, but the Duke of Bedford established a herd in England. In recent years, deer bred in captivity have been sent to China and reintroduced into a special reserve.

Rutting
For most of the year, red deer stags remain apart from the females, or hinds, and their young. During the breeding season, known as the rut, males collect harems of hinds which they vigorously defend by roaring or, if necessary, by fighting.

Breeding

Most species of antelope and deer give birth when the weather is fine and food is abundant. Young caribou are born in early June when the herd is migrating. The calves can follow their mother within minutes of birth. The young of some species are left alone. Their mothers come to suckle and clean them several times a day, until they are strong enough to join the herd.

Caribou
The Eurasian reindeer and the North American caribou are the same species. They live in large herds and migrate long distances every year to find food. The reindeer has been semi-domesticated by, among others, the Lapps of north Europe.

Female reindeer are the only female deer that grow antlers.

Females in a herd give birth within two weeks of each other.

A calf can run with the herd when only an hour old.

A reindeer calf weighs about 4 kg (9 lb) at birth.

Reindeer with calf

Antelope habitats

Antelopes are found in most kinds of tropical and subtropical habitats. Most are creatures of the open plains and forests, but others have adapted to live in deserts, wetlands, and mountains. Grazing antelopes live where there is plenty of grass, whereas the browsers tend to inhabit woodlands and forests.

Woodland inhabitant
Also called the chousingha, the shy, solitary four-horned antelope lives in wooded, hilly country. Hunting has greatly reduced its numbers, but it still survives in several wildlife reserves in India, and one reserve in Nepal.

Sitatunga hoof

Swamp inhabitant
The sitatunga lives only in swamps and marshes. It has evolved long hooves that help it to walk on marshy ground. When danger threatens, it submerges itself in water leaving only its nostrils exposed.

Pointed antler

Muntjak head

Tusk-like teeth

Muntjak skull

Defence

Some deer and antelope, the larger species in particular, may sometimes use their antlers and horns to defend themselves, although generally antlers and horns are not strong enough for defence. Most deer and antelopes rely on their excellent eyesight and acute sense of hearing to detect potential enemies, and on speed to escape from any predators that attack.

Self-defence
If attacked, a muntjak's first defence is to run away. If this fails, males thrash with their antlers. These are mounted on "stalks" of bone as long as the antlers themselves. Males also have two tusk like teeth used mainly in fighting rivals.

Pronking
The springbok of Africa can run fast to escape a predator. Like most gazelles, it will often leap high into the air, with legs stiff, hooves close together, and back arched. Called pronking, or stotting, this action may confuse predators, raise the alarm, or simply give the gazelle a better view.

Camouflage
Some deer and antelope avoid predators because they blend into their surroundings. Kirk's dik-dik is an African antelope that lives in dry bush country, where the thorny thickets protect it.

Red Deer

Scientific name	*Cervus elaphus*
Order	Artiodactyla
Family	Cervidae
Distribution	Europe and Asia. Introduced into Australia, New Zealand, and South America
Habitat	Woodland and open country
Diet	Grass, leaves, shoots, flowers (it both grazes and browses)
Size	Height at the shoulder: 1.4 m (4 ft 6 in)
Lifespan	12–15 years

African Wildlife
Buffalo and Other Wild Cattle
Grassland Wildlife

DENMARK

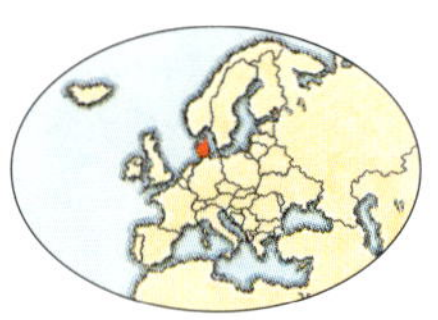

THE SMALLEST, flattest, and most southerly country in Scandinavia, Denmark occupies the Jylland peninsula, the islands of Sjaelland, Lolland, Falster, and Fyn, and more than 500 smaller islands. The Faeroe Islands and Greenland in the North Atlantic are self-governing Danish territories. A prosperous, environmentally conscious, and liberal nation, Denmark offers its people a high standard of living and was one of the first countries to set up a welfare system in the 1930s.

Physical features

Denmark's flat landscape is broken by low, rolling hills and gentle valleys with shady beech forests. There are also extensive areas of heathland, a beautiful lake district, and a coastline of cliffs, dunes, and broad sandy beaches.

DENMARK FACTS

CAPITAL CITY Copenhagen

AREA 43,094 sq km (16,639 sq miles)

POPULATION 5,300,000

MAIN LANGUAGE Danish

MAJOR RELIGION Christian

CURRENCY Danish krone

LIFE EXPECTANCY 76 years

PEOPLE PER DOCTOR 294

GOVERNMENT Multi-party democracy

ADULT LITERACY 99%

Jylland (Jutland)

The Jylland peninsula makes up about 70 per cent of Denmark's land. Its west coast is edged with beaches and the southwest has a sandy plain. Strong winds sweeping across the land drive windmills for generating electricity.

Baltic islands

The steep, chalk cliffs on the Baltic island of Møn contrast with the gentle dunes on other islands. The Danish take great care of their environment and beaches.

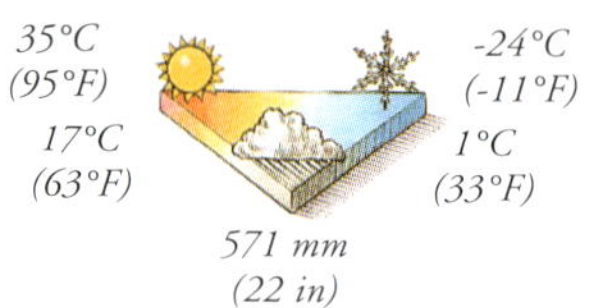

Climate

Denmark's usually mild and damp climate is dominated by stiff westerly winds. In many coastal areas, to prevent sand from the dunes from blowing over the land, the Danes have planted conifers as windbreaks.

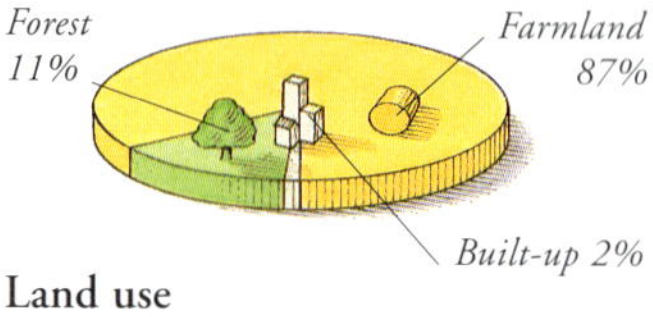

Forest 11%

Farmland 87%

Built-up 2%

Land use

Over four-fifths of Denmark is farmland, including lush pasture for grazing cattle and for raising pigs. Denmark's land yields few natural resources, although high winds are harnessed to produce power.

People

Only four per cent of the population is foreign – mainly Europeans. The only minority groups are Turks and Inuits from Greenland. The Danish have liberal policies on homosexuality and marriage, with a high divorce rate. Today, 47 per cent of all children are raised by unmarried couples or single parents. Three-quarters of all women work, and Denmark has the best child-support system in the world.

Danish family visiting Legoland on Jylland

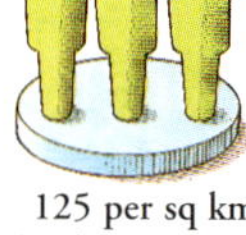

125 per sq km (324 per sq mile)

85% Urban

15% Rural

Danish pigs

Farming and industry

Danish farming is efficient and often run by co-operatives. Only about four per cent of the work-force is employed in farming, mainly of dairy cattle and pigs, yet agriculture accounts for much of the country's export income. Denmark also has successful fishing, manufacturing, and food industries for processing bacon and dairy products. Service industries employ 79 per cent of workers.

Copenhagen

Denmark's capital is also its most important port and Scandinavia's largest city. Criss-crossed with a network of canals, quaint alleys, and cycle paths, Copenhagen has many historic buildings and churches. It also boasts the Tivoli Gardens, an amusement park that attracts millions every year.

Tourist boat on canal

FIND OUT MORE: ATLANTIC OCEAN · ENERGY · EUROPE · EUROPE, HISTORY OF · EUROPEAN UNION · FARMING · FOOD · SCANDINAVIA, HISTORY OF · TRADE AND INDUSTRY · VIKINGS

DESERTS

FEW PLACES ON EARTH are as stark and hostile as a desert. Deserts are vast areas where very little rain falls – typically under 100 mm (3.9 inches) a year. Any rain that does fall quickly evaporates. Few plants can survive, and soil cannot develop in such a dry and barren or arid environment. The landscape is bare sand, gravel, or rock. Clear skies and sparse vegetation leave the ground exposed to extremes of temperature. In the tropics, cloudless skies create hot deserts with daytime temperatures which are often over 50°C (122°F). Deserts at higher latitudes can be extremely cold.

Areas thought to be at risk of desertification (shown in orange)

Twelve per cent of land is desert.

Desert regions

The world's great deserts lie deep within continents far from the moisture of the oceans. They are also along the Tropics of Cancer and Capricorn, on either side of the Equator, where sinking air creates stable dry weather.

Desert landforms and dunes

Strong winds, sudden flash floods, and exposure to extreme temperatures create distinctive desert features. The wind piles sand up in dunes or sand-blasts rocks. Flash floods carve canyon-like valleys. The desert heat creates corrosive chemicals which sculpt rocks into bizarre shapes.

Butte – eroded mesa

Wadi – gorge-like, generally dry valley

Mesa – isolated, flat-topped, steep-sided mountain

Parabolic dunes are also common on coasts.

Seif dunes form where sand is sparse and wind comes from two directions.

Oasis is a pocket of water.

Zeugen rocks are produced by weathering.

Hamada is an area strewn with boulders and stones.

Eroded arch

Playa is a dry lake bed of salt.

Bolson is a drainage basin.

Barchan dune is shaped like a crescent and its tips usually point downwind.

Transverse dune – ridge lying across the wind

Bajada is a slope of sand deposited by rivers along mountain edges.

Oasis

An oasis, such as the Azraq oasis in Jordan (above), is a fertile area within a desert that lies near an underground stream or a spring. Crops such as date palms can grow and desert dwellers can live supported by the land. Artificial oases can be created through irrigation.

Mirage

Sometimes the desert heat is so intense that desert travellers believe that they can see water. This is an optical illusion (a trick of the eye), caused by the reflection of a faraway object, which may give the false appearance of a sheet of water.

Types of deserts

Climatic conditions create different types of deserts. In Africa, the Sahara has vast areas of erg (sand seas), hamada (stony plateaus), reg (pebble plains), rocky deserts, canyons, and cliff deserts. In the Antarctic there are ice deserts, while in the deserts of the western USA the heat evaporates rain so quickly that it leaves behind dissolved minerals in a hard, salty crust.

Sandy desert

In flat areas, vast sand seas, or ergs, develop. After a rainfall, water rushes along a wadi, a dry river bed. The sandstone cliffs on either side are gradually worn away by the heat, wind, and rain.

Rocks brought to desert by flood water.

Rocky desert

Many of the world's deserts are strewn with boulders that have been washed there by flash flooding. These rocks are gradually broken down by the action of wind and weather.

The shifting desert

As climatic conditions change, deserts shrink and expand. In the past, the Sahel, the southern margin of the Sahara, was watered by summer rains moving up from the south. In recent years, the lack of rain in the Sahel has caused drought and famine in places such as Sudan and Ethiopia.

Desertification

The effect of drought and heavy grazing by cattle, sheep, and goats destroys vegetation cover, turning the area permanently to desert. This process is known as desertification.

FIND OUT MORE: CLIMATE · DESERT WILDLIFE · ECOLOGY AND ECOSYSTEMS · ROCKS AND MINERALS · WEATHER

DESERT WILDLIFE

THE DRIEST PLACES ON EARTH are known as deserts. Food is scarce, and there is little shelter from the sun and wind. Deserts are among the most inhospitable of all places in which to live. In spite of this, many remarkable animals survive and even thrive in these hostile surroundings. Birds, mammals, insects, arachnids, amphibians, and reptiles are all represented, together with some equally remarkable plants.

Deserts

Many different types of desert exist in different parts of the world. Some are mountainous and rocky; others are pebbly or full of sand dunes. Some become baking hot by day; others have bitterly cold winters.

Sahara
Stretching across North Africa, the Sahara is the greatest of all deserts. It is a vast wilderness of sand and rock, with only scattered palms and bushes to offer shade from the searing daytime sun. Most of the animals that live there find shelter under rocks or in burrows.

Oases
Oases provide reliable sources of drinking water for wildlife in the desert. They form in the few places where springs bubble up from underground, or where rainwater from neighbouring mountains collects in hollows.

Birds

Though some desert-dwelling doves and finches forage for seeds, the most well-known birds of arid lands are predators. They probe vegetation and scour the ground for prey, obtaining all the moisture they need from the bodies of their victims.

Gila woodpecker
The Gila woodpecker forages for insects in the deserts of Mexico and the USA. Typically, it hammers out nest-holes in the stems of large cacti.

Roadrunner
Roadrunners seldom fly, but they are extremely fast, agile runners. They often prey on desert snakes, which they subdue with a series of lethal stabs from their sharp beaks.

Falcons can spot prey from a great height.

Lanner falcon
This darting bird of prey nests among rocks and cliffs in the Sahara. It hunts small birds, which it chases and snatches in mid-air or on the ground. It also preys on smaller animals, such as gerbils, lizards, and locusts.

Mammals

Desert mammals show a remarkable ability to cope with conditions that would be dangerously hot and dry for most animals. Some, such as camels, can tolerate steep rises in their body temperature and long periods of dehydration. Others have special means of securing shade, obtaining moisture, finding food, and avoiding danger in the wide-open terrain.

Dwarf hamster
Only about 8.5 cm (3.3 in) long, this hamster lives in the deserts of Mongolia, Siberia, and China. It has thick fur, which helps to keep it warm in the bitterly cold winters.

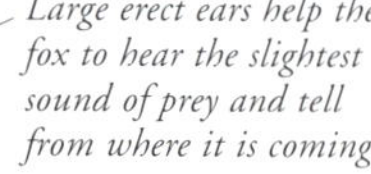

Pale-coloured fur reflects heat.

Large erect ears help the fox to hear the slightest sound of prey and tell from where it is coming.

Long, bushy tail can be curled around the body to keep it warm during the night.

Fennec fox
The fennec fox is small with large pointed ears. The large size of the ears helps the fox lose excess heat from its body during the heat of the day. The fox has dense fur, which keeps it warm on cold nights.

Red kangaroo
In Australian deserts, red kangaroos browse on bushes. They produce dry dung as a way of saving moisture, but still make regular trips to waterholes to replace moisture lost through sweating.

Kalahari ground squirrel
These burrowing rodents eat seeds and other plant material in the Kalahari Desert of Africa. During the day, they hold their bushy tails over their bodies for shade.

Bactrian camel
Camels are perfectly adapted for life in deserts. They can roam about for days without drinking or sweating. The two humps of the Bactrian camel act as fat reserves, off which the animal can live. The shaggy coat protects the camel during the cold winters in Asia's Gobi Desert.

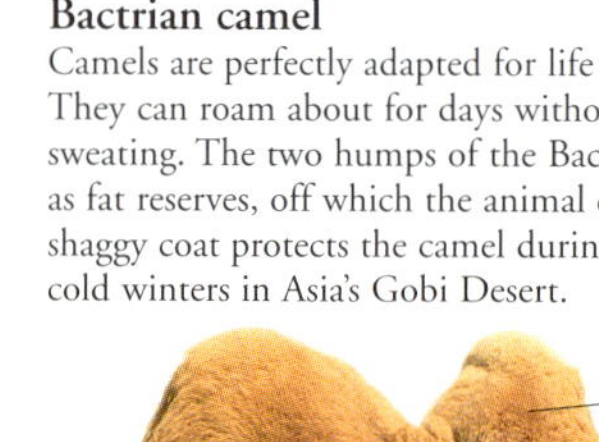

Humps flop over when the fat is depleted.

Long fur covers the upper surface of the feet.

D

Reptiles and amphibians

Both snakes and lizards are tolerant of dry climates, and these reptiles are among the most common of desert animals. Amphibians are much more in danger of drying out, but a few species do appear on the desert surface, especially after rare bouts of rain.

Sand viper buries itself tail first.

Snake descends vertically into the sand.

Sand viper

The sand viper has perfected an efficient way of disappearing on desert dunes. It wriggles down into the loose sand, becoming buried within seconds. It does this to escape danger and to be ready to attack prey.

Fringe-toed lizard

This lizard forages in sandy deserts. When the surface becomes too hot, it stands on two legs to help keep cool. Projections between its toes spread its weight and stop it from sinking into the sand.

Lizard can close its nostrils to prevent sand getting into its air passsages.

Water-holding frog

For months, this frog lies dormant underground in a waterproof cocoon. It emerges to feed and breed only after heavy rains, swelling its body with water before it returns into the soil.

Smooth scales

Sandfish

The sandfish is a lizard that makes its home on desert sand dunes. It is named after the way it moves across and through the sand, pushing sideways with its flattened toes as if it were swimming. Like other small lizards, it hunts mainly for insects.

Gila monster

The Gila monster is a fearsome lizard. Large, with a venomous bite, it leaves its burrow at dawn to hunt rodents and raid birds' nests. Fat stored in its thick tail provides nourishment when prey is scarce.

Yucca moth

The yucca moth of American deserts has evolved a close relationship with the yucca plant. The moth pollinates the plant; the yucca flowers give shelter to the moth larvae.

Desert cricket

An inhabitant of the deserts of India and Pakistan, the desert cricket can bury itself quickly in the sand. It digs a hole directly beneath itself with its star-shaped feet and sinks down.

Invertebrates

Few insects and other invertebrates can withstand the full force of the desert Sun. Those that can have an especially tough, waxy covering, or cuticle, that prevents them from drying out. Other invertebrates take shelter during the day.

White spots warn off predators.

Domino beetle

This domino beetle lives in the dry lands of northern Africa through to the Middle East. During the day, it hides under rocks and in holes made by other animals. At night, it emerges to hunt insects and other small prey.

Scorpion

Scorpions are among the hardiest of desert invertebrates, able to tolerate strong sunshine though they normally hunt at night. Armed with strong claws and a lethal sting, they ambush foraging insects such as locusts, as well as spiders and other scorpions.

The venom of this scorpion is strong enough to kill a person.

The scorpion holds its prey in its large claws.

Plants

Only the hardiest of drought-resistant plants can survive all year in the desert. Among these are cacti and yuccas. Seeds of more fragile plants lie dormant in the soil. After a rainburst, they sprout and flower before the moisture evaporates.

Seeds develop after the vine's flower has been pollinated by insects.

Little snapdragon vine

Rains in the Mexican desert bring the seeds of snapdragon vines to life. The vines quickly grow, trailing over the soil and curling around other plants. They flower and set new seed before they die as the conditions get dry again.

Desert holly

Some desert plants, such as the desert holly, have dusty-looking leaves. Salt secreted through leaf pores forms a fine whitish powder. This reflects some of the Sun's rays, helping to keep the leaves cool and preventing excessive evaporation of moisture.

Cacti

Many different kinds of cactus grow in American deserts. All store water in their green swollen stems. They do not have leaves, and this prevents excess moisture loss. Sharp spines deter animals from biting the succulent stems.

Welwitschia

This plant has two ribbon-like leaves that trail across the sand. Each leaf has millions of pores that extract moisture from the sea fogs that sweep the Namib Desert in Africa.

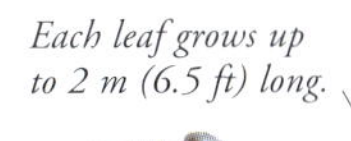

Each leaf grows up to 2 m (6.5 ft) long.

A welwitschia plant may live for 1,000 years or more.

Leaves usually split into several strips.

FIND OUT MORE
AFRICAN WILDLIFE | AMPHIBIANS | ASIAN WILDLIFE | BIRDS | BIRDS OF PREY | DESERTS | INSECTS | MAMMALS | PLANTS | REPTILES

DESIGN

ORIGINALLY A DESIGN was an artist's first sketch for a work of art; today, design plays a broader role in our lives. Before any object can be made, it must be designed. Most things around us have been designed to carry out a particular job. The design of objects is known as product design. There are also many other areas of design, such as fashion, garden, interior, and graphic design. Changing tastes can result in popular design movements, such as art nouveau and Bauhaus.

Product design

In order to design an object, the designer has several factors to consider. He or she must select a shape that suits the object's purpose but also consider other factors, such as the material to be used, the cost of manufacture, the safety and durability of the product, and how it will finally look. Product design usually aims to be both functional and stylish.

This bottle's shape is easily recognizable.

A can's ringpull opening is designed to open easily.

Coca-Cola bottle

Classic design

Some product designs so successfully combine functionality with a strong sense of style that they are timeless. The distinctive shape of the Coca-Cola bottle, for example, is a classic design that has hardly changed since 1915.

Headlamps and bumpers are chrome.

Large steering wheel

The MGB is compact but stylish.

MGB Tourer

Classic cars

Some classic designs express certain ideals perfectly. The sleek lines of a sports-car's body, such as this MGB, are intended to suggest speed and freedom. Launched in 1962, the MGB became the best-selling single model sports car ever, with 512,000 owners worldwide.

The design process

The first stage in the design process is writing a design brief which details the functions and features to be achieved in the finished object. The designer then does a first sketch. This is translated into a rough model, or prototype, which is repeatedly tested and revised as needed. The design process of making numerous small amendments is called an iterative process. Finally, the actual product is made.

1 The designer does a first sketch on a drawing board or computer. This sketch shows a vacuum cleaner.

This prototype is shaped out of hard foam.

Early prototype

2 A series of prototypes is made out of different materials to test aspects of the design. The final prototype is handmade and painted to look identical to the final product.

The plastic casing is very strong and light.

Dust collects in this area.

Long nozzle

Large back wheels for manoeuvring

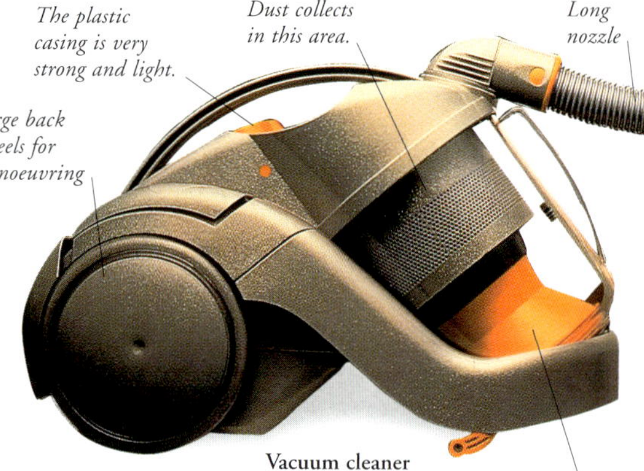

Vacuum cleaner

This vacuum cleaner uses a unique cyclone system to pick up dirt.

3 The final product is made to the revised design brief. Designs can be patented (protected by copyright law) to prevent someone copying an original design.

Graphic design

Graphic designers use words and images to communicate a strong visual message. We are surrounded by graphic design, in magazines and books, on posters, on street signs. Designers use letters in different sizes and typefaces, often with colours and patterns, to make an impact.

London Underground map

The London Underground map is a brilliant piece of design. By distorting the distances between stations, it is possible to see the entire London Underground at a glance.

Shell Oil logo

Logos

Logos are graphic designs that aim to communicate a message without words. Companies design logos to be easily recognized by the public. The simple shape and strong colours of the logo shown above advertise the Shell Oil Company worldwide.

Computer-aided design

Increasingly, much of the design process is carried out on computer. Using computer-aided design, the designer creates a three-dimensional model, such as a car, on screen which can then be rotated and viewed from all angles.

Art Nouveau

Design movements are trends in design, some of which have a lasting influence. Art Nouveau was a design movement beginning in Europe in the 1880s that aimed to make ordinary objects, such as buildings, furniture, and jewellery, beautiful.

This Art Nouveau window in Paris, France, shows typical decorative curves based on organic forms.

Walter Gropius

In 1919, the German architect Walter Gropius (1883–1969) founded the Bauhaus design school. It taught the importance of functional design and of using materials such as steel, glass, and concrete. Bauhaus influenced the development of the arts. Gropius (on right) is shown with the French architect, Le Corbusier (1887–1965).

FIND OUT MORE

ARCHITECTURE · ART, HISTORY OF · BUILDING AND CONSTRUCTION · CARS AND TRUCKS · CLOTHES AND FASHION · FURNITURE · GARDENS · PAINTING AND DRAWING · PRINTING · TRADE AND INDUSTRY

DICKENS, CHARLES

CHARLES DICKENS IS one of the greatest writers in the English language. He was a household name in his own lifetime. His lively descriptions of 19th-century Britain combine a superb gift for depicting people and their eccentricities with a social conscience, and compassion for the problems faced by ordinary people. He brought to the English novel the ability to portray an entire society in one book. His novels are still loved by readers of all ages.

Early life

Charles Dickens was born in Portsmouth, England, in 1812. His father was a clerk in the Royal Navy pay office and worked for a time in the royal dockyards in Chatham, Kent, where Charles spent much of his childhood. When his father was imprisoned for debt in London's Marshalsea Prison, Charles, then aged 12, had to take a series of menial jobs in factories and offices. He later used these painful experiences in some of his novels.

"Boz"

As a young man, Dickens was a journalist, covering Parliament for the *Morning Chronicle*. In 1833 he began to write a series of articles, mostly about London life, using the pseudonym "Boz". These were collected together in *Sketches by Boz* in 1836. Following their success, he was commissioned to write some humorous sporting stories. These appeared in 1836–37 as *The Posthumous Papers of the Pickwick Club* and made Dickens the most famous writer of his day.

Scrooge meets the Ghost of Christmas Past

David Copperfield

David Copperfield

In 1849–50 Dickens wrote *David Copperfield*, a partly autobiograpical novel in which he used his own experiences of an impoverished childhood and menial employment to great effect. Of all his books, it was Dickens' favourite. The novel features Mr Micawber, who is loosely based on Dickens' father. Always in debt, and always waiting for "something to turn up", Micawber is one of the great characters of English literature.

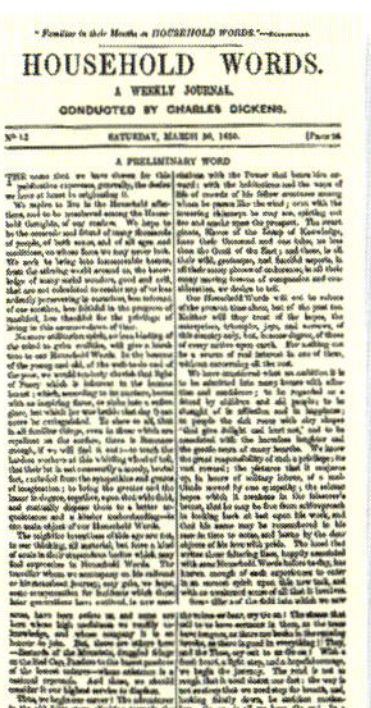

"Familiar in their Mouths as HOUSEHOLD WORDS."

HOUSEHOLD WORDS.

A WEEKLY JOURNAL.

CONDUCTED BY CHARLES DICKENS.

No 12 SATURDAY, MARCH 30, 1850.

A PRELIMINARY WORD

Household Words

From 1850, Dickens edited and contributed first to the magazine *Household Words*, and then, from 1859, to *All The Year Round*. He used these monthly magazines to publish his latest novel in installments, reaching a far wider readership than he would have done by simply publishing a book. Both magazines featured works by other famous writers of the time, such as Elizabeth Gaskell and Wilkie Collins. Dickens also included articles about the social problems of his time, such as poor housing and factory accidents.

A Christmas Carol

Ebenezer Scrooge, who refused to celebrate Christmas, and his impoverished clerk Bob Cratchit make *A Christmas Carol* (published in 1843) one of Dickens's most popular novels. Scrooge changes his ways when he witnesses a series of visions, including his own death and the ghosts of Christmas Past, Present, and Future.

In a scene from *Oliver Twist*, Oliver asks for more porridge.

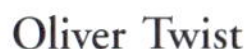

Oliver Twist

The story of Oliver tells of a pauper child of unknown parentage who was brought up in a workhouse and dared to ask for more food. *Oliver Twist* was first published as a book in 1838. The book was later made into a successful musical and film. The story was the first by Dickens to explore the dark side of London life in the 19th century, and the fact that thousands of children were living rough on the streets or in inhuman workhouses.

CHARLES DICKENS	
1812	Born in Portsmouth, England.
1824	Father imprisoned for debt.
1836	Marries Catherine Hogarth; publishes *Sketches by Boz.*
1836–7	*Pickwick Papers*
1838	*Oliver Twist*
1839	*Nicholas Nickleby*
1850	*David Copperfield*
1853	*Bleak House*
1857	*Little Dorrit*
1858	First reading tour
1859	*A Tale of Two Cities*
1861	*Great Expectations*
1864	*Our Mutual Friend*
1870	Dies and is buried in Westminster Abbey.

Dickensian London

In Dickens's time, London was a rich city at the centre of the biggest empire the world had ever seen. But many people lived in poverty, making a living from whatever work they could find. Dickens described their suffering, but he loved London – its sights, sounds, and smells feature in all his books.

Social reforms

Dickens often spoke in public about the plight of the poor, the need for educational reform, and the importance of good sanitation to remove the threat of disease. His speeches and novels helped to raise awareness of the need for radical reform, and led to many changes in the law.

London street, 19th century

Public readings

Dickens went on three tours of Britain and one of America, reading selections from his novels. He put vast amounts of energy into these readings, adapting his works specially for public performance, and reading aloud all the parts himself. In 1869, he began a fourth British tour, but his health began to fail, and he died the following year.

BOOKS · EMPIRES · INDUSTRIAL REVOLUTION · LITERATURE · UNITED KINGDOM, HISTORY OF · WRITING

DIGESTION

THE BODY NEEDS THE nutrients in food to grow, maintain its structure, and provide energy. But the food we eat cannot be used by the body until it is processed by the digestive system. This is essentially a long tube, running from mouth to anus. As food passes along the digestive system it is chewed, and crushed, and then broken down chemically by enzymes. As it passes along the small intestine, food resembles a thin soup, and simple food molecules can be absorbed into the body itself by way of the bloodstream.

Swallowing

Once food is chewed, the tongue pushes the ball of food, or bolus, to the back of the mouth. As it touches the throat, the bolus triggers a reflex action and passes into the oesophagus. A flap called the epiglottis closes the entrance to the trachea (windpipe) to stop food entering the lungs.

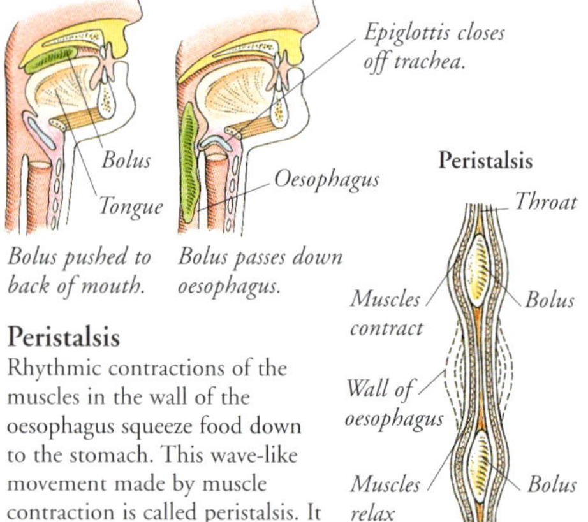

Bolus pushed to back of mouth.

Bolus passes down oesophagus.

Peristalsis

Rhythmic contractions of the muscles in the wall of the oesophagus squeeze food down to the stomach. This wave-like movement made by muscle contraction is called peristalsis. It also occurs in the small intestine.

Digestive process

The digestive process has four stages: ingestion, digestion, absorption, and egestion. Ingestion happens when you eat food and is followed by digestion. Absorption is the transfer of food molecules into the bloodstream and egestion is the removal of waste as faeces.

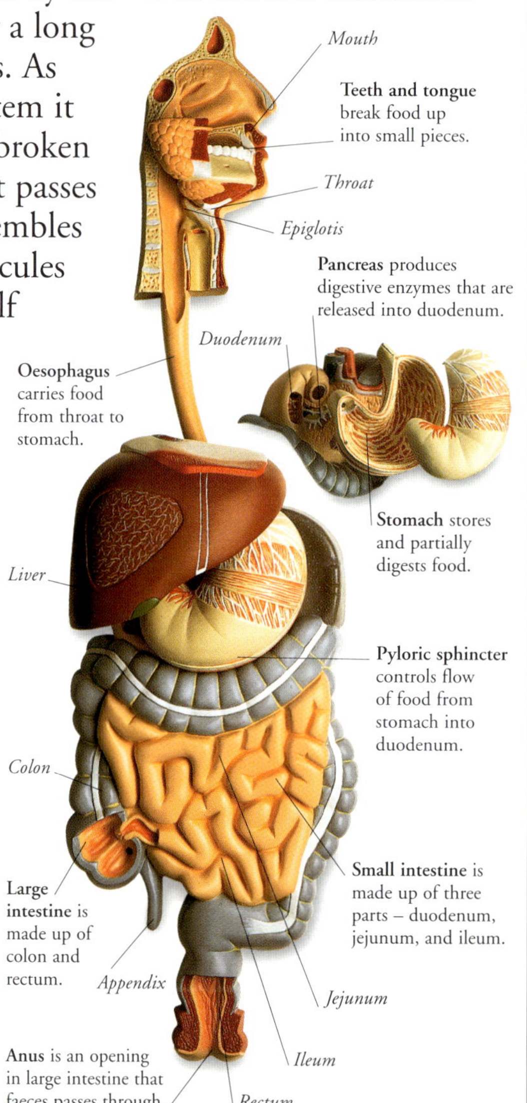

Teeth and tongue break food up into small pieces.

Pancreas produces digestive enzymes that are released into duodenum.

Oesophagus carries food from throat to stomach.

Stomach stores and partially digests food.

Pyloric sphincter controls flow of food from stomach into duodenum.

Small intestine is made up of three parts – duodenum, jejunum, and ileum.

Large intestine is made up of colon and rectum.

Anus is an opening in large intestine that faeces passes through.

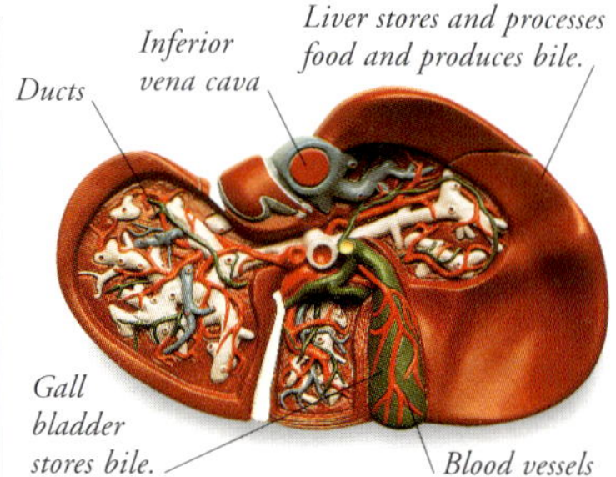

Liver, pancreas, and gall bladder

These three organs take part in digestion even though, since they have other body functions, they are not part of the digestive system. The liver produces bile, which is stored in the gall bladder and helps digest fats. The pancreas produces digestive enzymes that are released into the small intestine.

Absorption

Simple food molecules are absorbed into the bloodstream across the wall of the small intestine. Tiny finger-like projections called villi (singular: villus) greatly increase the surface area over which food can be absorbed.

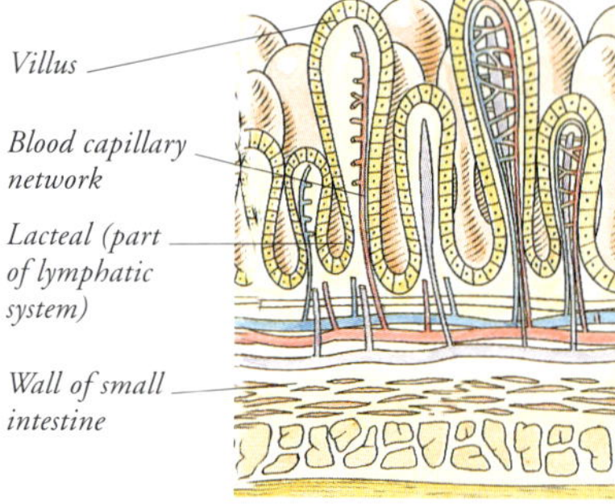

Imaging the intestine

A special liquid is introduced into the large intestine to show clearly its position and internal shape. This type of X-ray enables doctors to detect signs of disease inside the large intestine without having to operate.

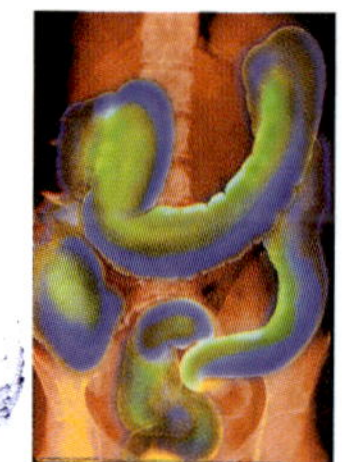

William Beaumont

The US Army surgeon William Beaumont (1785–1853) was the first to observe how food was digested in the stomach. In 1822, Beaumont treated a patient who had shot himself in the side and was left with an opening into his stomach. Through this opening, Beaumont was able to observe the stomach's movements during digestion and to record his findings.

Food and enzymes

Enzymes are biological catalysts that speed up the conversion of one substance into another. Digestive enzymes speed up the breakdown of the complex carbohydrates, fats, and proteins that make up most of our food.

Carbohydrates

The body's main fuel, carbohydrate, comes in the form of sugars and complex carbohydrates, which include starch. Enzymes break starchy foods down into sugars such as glucose.

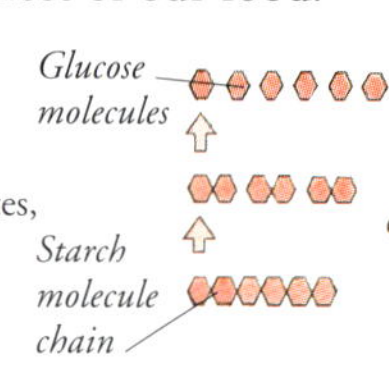

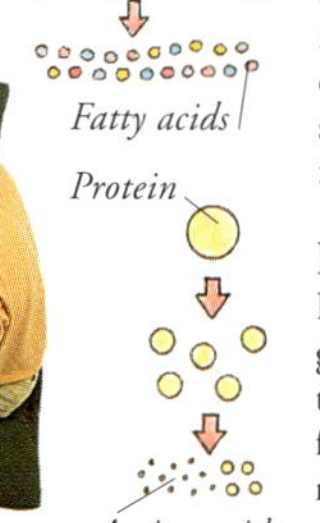

Fats

Fats provide the body with energy. Foods rich in fats include eggs and meat. Fats are broken down by enzymes in the small intestine to form fatty acids.

Proteins

Proteins are needed for growth and maintaining the body. Protein-rich foods are meat, fish, and nuts. Proteins are broken down into amino acids.

FIND OUT MORE
CHEMISTRY
FOOD
HORMONES AND ENDOCRINE SYSTEM
HUMAN BODY
IMMUNE AND LYMPHATIC SYSTEM
TEETH AND JAWS

DINOSAURS

FOR 150 MILLION YEARS, from the Triassic Period until the end of the Cretaceous Period, 65 million years ago, dinosaurs lived on Earth. Their remains have been discovered in every continent including Antarctica. They formed a varied group of land-living reptiles. People who study prehistoric life, called palaeontologists, divide them into two main groups – the Ornithischia and the Saurischia. There were meat-eating and plant-eating dinosaurs. Some dinosaurs, were huge; others were only the size of chickens.

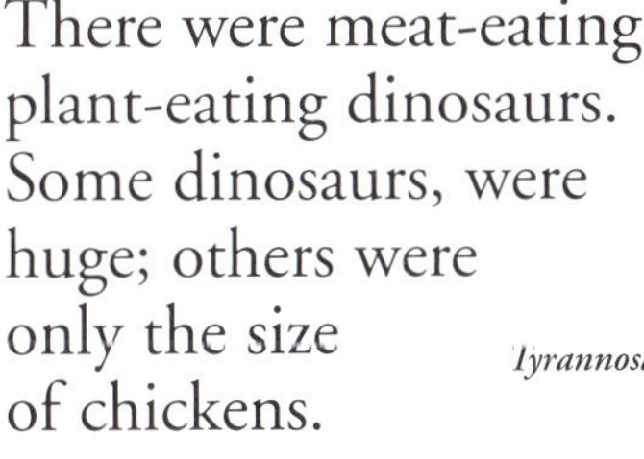

Tyrannosaurus

Iguanodon skull

Iguanodon skull
Gideon Mantell, an English doctor, named *Iguanodon* in 1825, noting the similarity between its teeth and those of the modern iguana. *Iguanodon*'s teeth were shaped to fit tightly together. They wore down as the dinosaur chewed its food of tough vegetation with the help of a hinged jaw.

Iguanodon tooth

Iguanodon
This was one of the first dinosaurs to be discovered. Modern reconstructions give it an outstretched tail and forelimbs that can reach the ground.

Iguanodon

Iguanodon foot

Ornithischians

The Ornithischia, or bird-hipped dinosaurs, such as *Iguanodon*, were all herbivorous. They had a huge number of teeth – *Corythosaurus* had 2,000 – and a hinged upper jaw that allowed them to chew.

Iguanodon foot
The feet of *Iguanodon* had small hooves on the toes instead of claws, and would have made recognizable three-toed prints with rounded digits. *Iguanodon* probably walked on its toes, which, therefore, had to be strong to carry the animal's great weight.

Saurischians

The Saurischia, or lizard-hipped dinosaurs, include the meat-eating theropods, which walked on two legs, such as *Tyrannosaurus*, and the plant-eating sauropods, which walked on four legs, such as *Diplodocus*. The sauropods were the largest ever land animals.

Tyrannosaurus tooth
Carnivorous dinosaurs had curved, pointed teeth. The sharp edges often had serrations, which helped the dinosaurs to slice through skin and meat Palaeontologists still have to be careful when handling these teeth.

Tyrannosaurus skeleton
Tyrannosaurus may have hunted as well as scavenged on other dinosaurs. It had a massive skull with powerful jaws, supported by a short, flexible neck. This flexibility allowed the animal to twist its head around to wrench flesh from its prey.

Tyrannosaurus *tore off the flesh of its prey with its teeth and claws.*

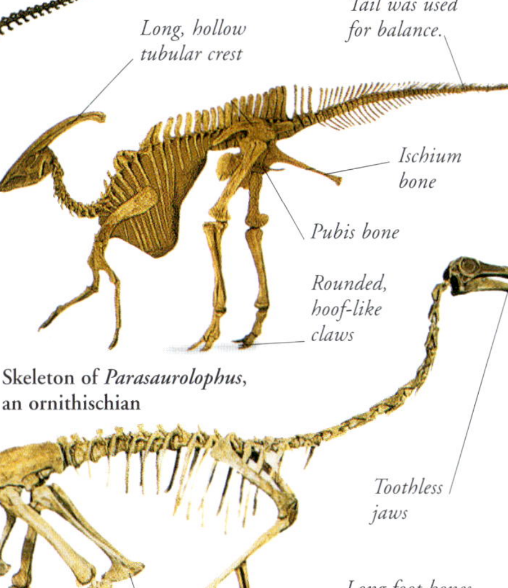

Skeleton of *Parasaurolophus*, an ornithischian

Skeleton of *Gallimimus*, a saurischian

Tyrannosaurus
Although not thought to be the largest of the carnivorous dinosaurs, *Tyrannosaurus* was still an extremely fearsome predator. It walked on its hind legs with its back level and head raised. It could run very fast, its tail balancing the weight of its huge heavy body.

Fossil dung
Preserved pieces of dung are called coprolites. They contain the remains of what dinosaurs ate, such as bone fragments, fish scales, or plant remains. Scientists can study these to find out about the diet of dinosaurs.

Hips
Dinosaurs fall into one of the two main groups, according to the structure of their hip bones. The bird-hipped dinosaurs (ornithischians), such as *Parasaurolophus*, had a pubis bone in their hip girdle that sloped backward, parallel to the ischium bone. The lizard-hipped dinosaurs (saurischians), such as *Gallimimus*, had a pubis bone that sloped forward away from the ischium.

***Orodromeus* nest**

The first dinosaurs

One of the earliest dinosaurs was *Eoraptor*, meaning "early plunderer". It was no bigger than a large dog and lived 225 million years ago (mya). As with all the early dinosaurs, it was a carnivore and walked on two legs.

***Eoraptor* skull**

Breeding

Dinosaurs laid hard-shelled eggs as some reptiles do today. Many dinosaurs laid a clutch of eggs in a hollowed-out nest in the ground. Several fossilized nests have been found close together, which suggests that some dinosaurs nested in colonies. The chicks developed rapidly and may have left the nest soon after hatching. Many were cared for by the parent dinosaur until they were able to look after themselves.

Richard Owen

Born in Lancaster, England, Richard Owen (1804–92) became the Hunterian Professor of the Royal College of Surgeons in 1836. As well as being an anatomist, he was a brilliant palaeontologist. He was the first to use the term "dinosaurs", which means "terrible lizards", in a report in 1842. He noted that these animals had pillar-like legs, rather than the sprawling legs of modern reptiles, and should be classified separately.

Defence

Dinosaurs protected themselves against attack from predators. Different dinosaurs developed a variety of powerful defences. For example, *Triceratops* had horns on its head, *Euoplocephalus* had a tail club, and *Tuojiangosaurus* had a spiky tail. Some of these adaptations may have had several functions, but one of them was likely to have been defence. Scientists cannot say exactly how these animals defended themselves, but it is easy to imagine.

Tuojiangosaurus

The flanks and belly of *Tuojiangosaurus* were vulnerable to attack. Near the tip of its tail were four bony spikes. These pointed up and outwards, producing a formidable defence when the dinosaur swung its tail. This animal was a type of bird-hipped dinosaur called a stegosaur. It lived in China 157-145 mya.

Tuojiangosaurus

All stegosaurs had a double row of plates running down their back.

Small narrow head with a walnut-sized brain

Short front limbs

Defensive spikes

Reconstruction of *Iguanodon* hand

Thumb spike

Iguanodon spike

When *Iguanodon* was first reconstructed, its large spike was placed on its beak. It is now known that the spike was on its thumb and may have been used as a defensive weapon against predators. The spike could have pierced the belly, throat, or eye of an attacker. The dinosaur may also have used it in fights for status with other *Iguanodons*, and even to help it feed.

Raised nodules for protection

Dinosaur skin

Occasionally, the skin, or skin impression, of dinosaurs is preserved. From these fossils we can tell that the skin of many dinosaurs was not smooth, but nodular and rough. This would have given some protection against the claws and teeth of predators. This is the skin of *Polacanthus*.

Euoplocephalus *had thick bone plates and spikes over its back, with a large shoulder spike for added protection.*

Claw

Euoplocephalus

Club was made out of several bones fused together.

Euoplocephalus

This armoured ornithischian had a large bony club at the tip of its muscular tail. It could have swung this with great force, disabling a predator.

Brow horn

Frill anchored the jaw muscles.

Nose horn

***Triceratops* skull – side view**

Triceratops

The ceratopsians, or horned dinosaurs, were ornithischians. Most of them had brow horns and nose horns. *Triceratops*, the largest ceratopsian, had two long horns on its brow, a short nose horn, and also a bony neck frill protecting its neck. Its head took up nearly one-third of its length. It probably used its horns to fend off predators, and males used them to deter rivals in the herd, mostly by display, but also by fighting.

***Triceratops* skull – front view**

Dinosaur discoveries

Removing dinosaur fossils from surrounding rock is tricky. Some need to be protected in a jacket made of plaster or polyurethane foam before they are taken to a laboratory. Fossils are found every year, and each discovery teaches us more about these extinct animals.

Finding dinosaur bones.

FIND OUT MORE

ANIMALS | ANIMAL BEHAVIOUR | EVOLUTION | FOSSILS | PREHISTORIC LIFE | REPTILES | SKELETON

Dinosaurs

Ornithischians

Heterodontosaurus was one of the first bird-hipped dinosaurs. It lived about 205 mya.

Corythosaurus had a tall crest on its head.

Iguanodon could walk on two or four legs.

Styracosaurus was a short-frilled ceratopsian.

Scelidosaurus was the oldest-known armoured dinosaur.

Hypsilophodon was once thought to have lived in trees, but its limbs were not built for climbing.

Stegoceras was a pachycephalosaur, and had a thick-domed skull.

Stegosaurus was the largest stegosaur at 9 m (30 ft) long. It had large plates along its back.

Euoplocephalus had body armour and a tail club to protect it against attack.

Saurischians

Deinonychus was a meat eater and may have hunted in packs.

Gallimimus was shaped like an ostrich and was one of the fastest running dinosaurs.

Dilophosaurus had two high crests on top of its large head.

Baryonyx had a huge 30-cm (12-in)-long claw on each hand.

Anchisaurus may have eaten both meat and plants.

Compsognathus was small – only 74 cm (2.5 ft) long.

Herrerasaurus was a carnivore that lived in Argentina 228 mya.

Barosaurus resembled *Diplodocus*. It was about the same size with a shorter tail and longer neck.

Tyrannosaurus was one of the largest known land-living carnivores, weighing up to 6 tonnes.

DISEASES

JUST LIKE A MACHINE, the human body works smoothly and efficiently most of the time. However, it may occasionally stop operating normally. This may be due to an injury, such as a broken bone, but, more commonly, it is caused by a disease. Diseases occur because the body has been infected by a pathogen (germ), as in the case of influenza or food poisoning, or because of problems arising inside the body, such as heart disease or diabetes. Some diseases can be controlled and defeated by the body's immune system. More serious diseases may need drug treatment or surgery in order to cure them.

Epidemiologist tests samples in laboratory.

Epidemiology

Epidemiology is the study of diseases as they affect groups of people. Epidemiologists are concerned with why diseases occur in a population, and their control and prevention. They have discovered links between disease and diet, environmental factors, and lifestyle. Epidemiologists first discovered the link between smoking and lung cancer.

Non-infectious diseases

If a disease is non-infectious, it is not caused by a pathogen and cannot be passed from one person to another. Non-infectious diseases include circulatory system diseases, such as heart attacks, strokes, and cancer, and respiratory diseases, such as bronchitis and emphysema.

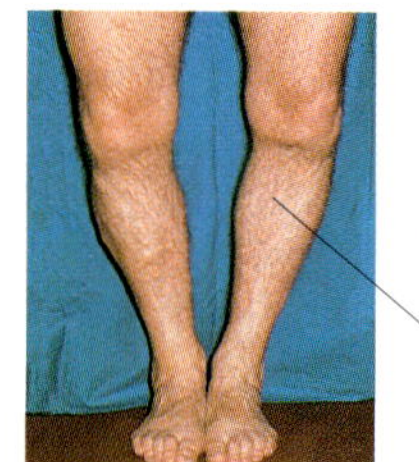

Rickets may leave sufferer with bow-legs.

Nutritional diseases

Nutritional diseases are caused by a lack of a balanced diet, causing a deficiency of vitamins and minerals. A child not getting enough vitamin D may suffer from rickets, where the skeleton does not form properly.

Industrial diseases

Work situations may affect a person's health. Industrial processes can create harmful environments or use chemicals that cause diseases. Some miners develop a lung disease called pneumoconiosis.

Miners may develop lung problems.

Infectious diseases

Infectious diseases are those, such as the common cold or pneumonia, that are caused by pathogens that invade the body. The most common pathogens are bacteria and viruses, although some diseases, such as thrush, are caused by fungi, and some, such as malaria, by tiny organisms called protists. They are normally destroyed by the body's immune system. Those that are not can often be dealt with by drugs.

Chickenpox causes an itchy rash that, when scratched, can leave scars.

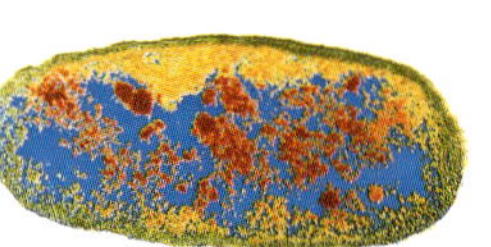

Bacteria are in water, air, and soil, as well as many plant and animal tissues.

Bacteria

Bacteria are single-celled micro-organisms. Most bacteria are not harmful to humans. However, some multiply inside the body and produce toxins that cause disease. Bacterial diseases include typhoid and scarlet fever. Most can be treated with drugs called antibiotics.

Viruses

Viruses are tiny infective particles, not usually classed as living things. They take over a body cell's genetic material (DNA) and make copies of themselves that infect other cells. Human viral infections include colds, measles, and HIV.

HIV and AIDS

The human immunodeficiency virus, or HIV, causes AIDS (Acquired Immune Deficiency Syndrome). HIV infects and destroys the cells that form part of the body's immune system – the body's defences against diseases. HIV is transmitted by some bodily fluids, such as blood and semen. The system becomes progressively weaker, and the person becomes infected with various diseases, known collectively as AIDS.

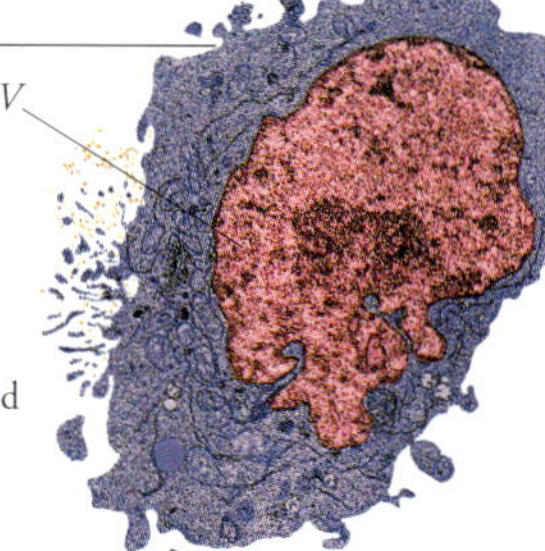

HIV

Spreading infection

Most diseases are acquired from other people by skin-to-skin contact, breathing in droplets when someone sneezes or coughs, or by sexual contact without the use of condoms. Infection can also be spread through infected food, contaminated water, and insect bites. Drug users who share needles risk infections of the blood, such as hepatitis and HIV.

Sanitation

Human faeces contain bacteria and viruses that cause disease. If there is poor sanitation and human waste is discharged into rivers, people may catch diseases such as dysentery or cholera through contact with polluted water.

Keeping rivers clean prevents diseases that can be caught if people drink, wash, or grow food in the water.

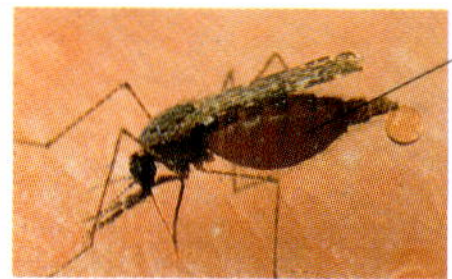

Some mosquitoes carry strains of malaria that are resistant to drugs.

Insects

Insects such as mosquitoes and fleas feed on human blood and can carry disease. A mosquito transmits the malaria micro-organism if it feeds on an infected person's blood.

Preventing disease

Disease prevention is an important part of modern medicine. Diseases can be prevented by better sanitation, immunization, and improving food hygiene. Eating a balanced diet and exercising may also prevent disease.

Syringes that are not properly sterilized after use can spread disease.

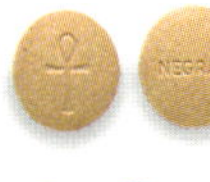

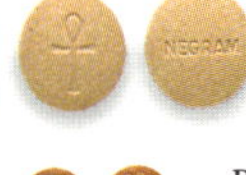

Pills contain measured amounts of drugs.

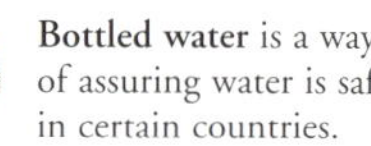

Bottled water is a way of assuring water is safe in certain countries.

FIND OUT MORE

BLACK DEATH · CELLS · CURIE, MARIE · DRUGS · HUMAN BODY · IMMUNE AND LYMPHATIC SYSTEM · PASTEUR, LOUIS

DISNEY, WALT

IN 1901, A MAN WAS BORN who would change the face of entertainment. Walt Disney became interested in animation as a schoolboy; by the time he was 20 he was making short animated films. But it was his later work that changed the history of the cinema. He created a string of cartoon characters which have been favourites ever since – Donald Duck, Goofy, and, above all, Mickey Mouse. Walt Disney also made the first feature-length animated film, *Snow White and the Seven Dwarfs* (1937), which was followed by many other screen successes.

Early life

In 1906, Disney's father Elias bought a farm at Marceline, Missouri. This was where young Walt first saw animals at close quarters. He also became interested in drawing. The first he ever sold was a drawing of the local doctor's stallion, for which the doctor paid Disney a nickel.

Early animation
Disney began to make animated films in 1920. These films featured characters which were made by cutting figures out of paper. The figures could be moved while they were photographed with a hand-cranked camera.

Disney with a hand-cranked camera

Hollywood

Disney moved to Hollywood in 1923. There were no animation studios, so he set up his own. He was soon in the forefront of technical innovation, pioneering the use of synchronized sound and the three-colour Technicolor process.

Mickey Mouse
Steamboat Willie, the first cartoon to feature Mickey Mouse, appeared in 1928. This was also the first cartoon with sound. Disney himself supplied Mickey's voice, and the film was an instant success. Mickey has since appeared in many other films. He has become the instantly recognizable Disney symbol and has appeared on countless Disney merchandise products.

Walt Disney with Mickey Mouse and Donald Duck

Snow White with the seven dwarfs

Snow White
In the 1920s, cartoons were normally shown before a full-length live-action film. But in 1935, Disney had the idea of producing a full-length cartoon, *Snow White and the Seven Dwarfs* (1937). Hundreds of animators worked on the film, which was followed by many other full-length animated features.

Mary Poppins
From the 1950s onwards, Disney produced many live-action films. Some of these, such as the musical fantasy *Mary Poppins* (1964), also included animated sequences.

Julie Andrews in a scene from *Mary Poppins*

The Disney Club
Disney was the first US major studio to create locally produced children's programming such as The Disney Club, and is the only studio to maintain a world-wide network of production offices. This network produces more than 40 weekly Disney programmes, which reach over 300 million viewers.

Disney Club logo

Disneyland

For many years, Walt Disney wanted to recreate the sets and characters of his films in a recreational park. The result, Disneyland, opened in 1955 in Anaheim, near Los Angeles, California. This theme park is one of the world's most popular attractions. Other parks have since opened: Walt Disney World in Florida and Disneyland ® Paris.

Disneyland

FIND OUT MORE
CARTOONS AND ANIMATION
FILMS AND FILM-MAKING
TELEVISION

WALT DISNEY

1901	Born in Chicago, USA.
1919	Begins to make animated films.
1923	Moves to Hollywood.
1928	*Steamboat Willie,* featuring Mickey Mouse.
1937	*Snow White and the Seven Dwarfs,* the first feature-length animated film.
1940	*Pinocchio.*
1940	*Fantasia.*
1942	*Bambi.*
1955	Disneyland opens.
1964	*Mary Poppins.*
1966	Walt Disney dies.

DOGS

DOGS HAVE LIVED with people for more than 12,000 years. They may have started to stay near humans for food and warmth. Then people began to train dogs to work for them. They bred certain types of dog for herding and guarding other domestic animals, then for hunting and for companionship. Gradually, different types of dog developed, but it was not until the end of the 19th century that specific breeds were classified. Today, there are about 200 dog breeds throughout the world. They are more varied in their appearance and behaviour than any other domestic animal.

Siberian husky

English setter

Shetland sheepdogs

Chihuahua

Scottish terriers

Bloodhound

Dog groups

The people of ancient Egypt and western Asia were the first to breed distinct types of dog for different purposes. By Roman times, dogs were kept for much the same reasons as they are today. There are six main groups – (from left to right) top row: working, sporting, herding; bottom row: companion, terriers, and hounds.

Domestic dogs

All breeds of domestic dog, from the Great Dane to the chihuahua, are descended from the wolf and have inherited the wolf's instincts. Like wolves, dogs are pack animals. They treat humans as part of their pack, and can be trained to accept their owner as the pack leader, and to follow his or her commands.

Borzois have sharp eyesight and hunt by sight.

Long, strong legs and a flexible body for speed

The borzoi was bred in Russia in the 13th century and used first to hunt wolves.

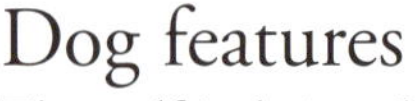

Dog features

The wolf is designed to chase, capture, kill, and eat its prey. It is agile, with strong legs for running long distances. Domestic dogs retain many of the features of a wolf, but through selective breeding now exist in many shapes, sizes, and colours.

Coats

There are three main types of dog coats – long, short, and wiry. Most breeds have an outer coat of guard hairs and an undercoat of shorter hairs. They moult, or shed their fur, changing their coat in spring and autumn.

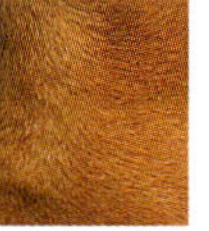
Short hair

Long hair

Wire hair

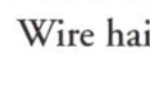

Feet

Dogs walk on their toes rather than the soles of their feet. Their paw pads help with grip, as do their claws, which are non-retractable.

Senses

Dogs have highly developed senses of hearing and smell. They use these in communication and to track down their prey. The police use dogs to sniff out explosives, criminals, and drugs. The dogs can see well in the dark and are good at seeing movement in the distance.

Beagles were bred to hunt hares.

Reproduction

A female dog is pregnant for about nine weeks, then gives birth to several puppies known as a litter. At birth, puppies are blind and deaf. Their eyes open at about 10 to 12 days old and they are able to hear at 13 to 17 days old. Teeth start to grow between three and five weeks of age.

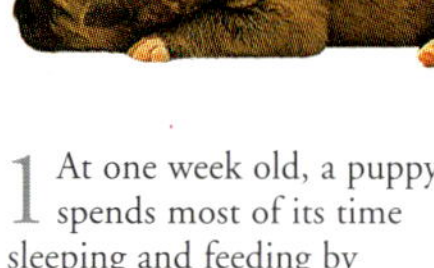
A young puppy is defenceless.

1 At one week old, a puppy spends most of its time sleeping and feeding by suckling from its mother.

All puppies are born with short legs and a little tail.

2 At two weeks old, the puppy takes its first wobbling steps and begins to explore. Its eyes are now open and it can hear.

Eyes are fully open.

3 At three weeks old, the puppy may start to eat solid food. At first, its mother will regurgitate meat for it.

4 At six weeks old, the puppy no longer feeds from its mother. It can soon be taken away from her to a new home.

FIND OUT MORE

ANIMALS · ANIMALS, BEHAVIOUR · CATS · GRASSLAND WILDLIFE · MAMMALS · POLICE · WOLVES AND WILD DOGS

Dogs

D

Working dogs

Great Dane makes an excellent family pet.

Mastiff existed in Britain in ancient Roman times.

Boxer is a lively and affectionate dog.

German shepherd dog is intelligent and enthusiastic.

Dalmatian, used to deter highwaymen in the 1800s.

St Bernard exists in wire- and smooth-haired forms.

Companion dogs

Papillon is named after the French for "butterfly".

Pekingese has a flattened face, with a broad nose.

Bulldog is a strong but affectionate dog.

Miniature poodle, world's most popular dog in the 1950s.

Cavalier King Charles spaniel, bred in 1900s.

Pug has a soft coat and a curled tail.

Terriers

Airedale terrier is the largest terrier breed.

Border terrier was first bred for hunting rats.

Staffordshire bull terrier is loyal and devoted.

Boston terrier originated in Boston, USA, in the 1800s.

Smooth fox terrier is alert and tireless.

Parson Jack Russell terrier has a mostly white coat.

Yorkshire terrier is a small but spirited guard dog.

Cairn terrier has a shaggy, water-resistant coat.

Australian terrier is capable of tackling a snake.

Hounds

Basset hound is an agile and single-minded hunter

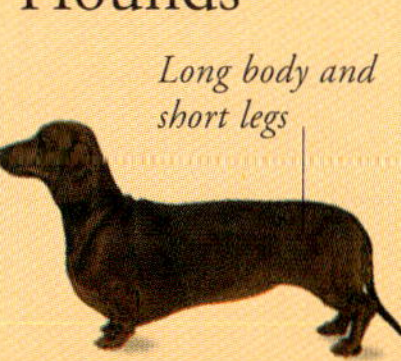

Dachshunds can be long-, smooth-, or wire-haired.

Whippet was bred in the 1800s for racing.

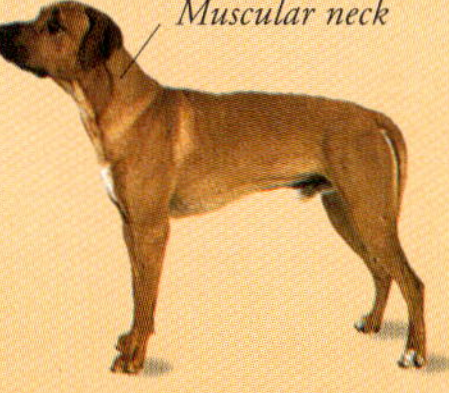

Rhodesian ridgeback has a ridge of hair on its back.

Afghan hound needs plenty of exercise.

Greyhound is built for speed.

Lurcher: individuals vary considerably within the breed.

Saluki, fast and agile, was once used to hunt gazelles.

Irish wolfhound is the tallest dog in the world.

Herding dogs

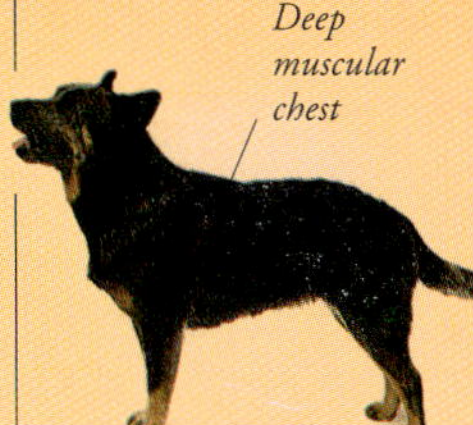

Australian cattle dog has great stamina.

Border collie is an outstanding sheepdog.

Old English sheepdog has a thick, shaggy coat.

Sporting dogs

Pointer is agile, athletic, and needs much exercise.

English springer spaniel is one of the largest spaniels.

Water-resistant coat

Curly-coated retriever is one of the oldest breeds.

DRAMA

DRAMA HAS BEEN DELIGHTING people for at least 2,500 years. A Broadway musical, a play by Shakespeare, and a television soap opera are all different sorts of drama. What they have in common is the presence of actors, who perform a story (the play) in a theatrical setting, to entertain an audience and make them think. Dramatists (writers of drama) use their art to entertain and thrill their audience or, more seriously, to explore human character and raise questions about the nature and meaning of life.

Early drama

Western drama originated in ancient Greece, where plays were staged to honour the gods. The Greeks invented two of the most enduring dramatic forms, tragedy and comedy, which were later imitated by the Romans.

Classical Greek drama

The ancient Greeks held regular drama festivals, at which dramatists competed for prizes. Their tragedies were based on characters from Greek mythology. Their comedies ranged in style from uproarious satires to more realistic dramas.

Statuette of muse, holding a mask from Greek comedy

Medieval drama

Western drama went into a decline at the end of the Roman Empire, but revived in the 10th century, with the rise of Christian religious drama. Amateur players produced plays enacting stories from the Bible, performed over a number of days. The audience watched out of doors, in market-places and other public spaces.

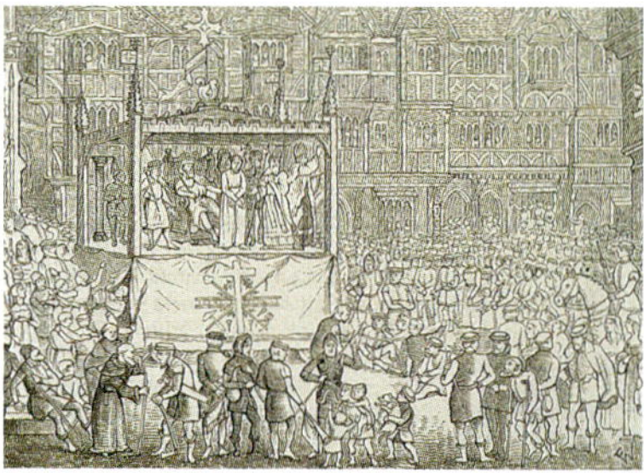

Religious drama, York, England, 13th century

Renaissance and 17th century

The traditions of ancient Greek drama were revived in Renaissance Italy and spread through Europe. Many plays were written in verse. Drama thrived in the 16th and 17th centuries, the age of English playwright William Shakespeare (1564–1616) and his contemporaries.

Lope de Vega

Phèdre **(1677), by Racine**

France

The French dramatist Jean Racine (1639–99) wrote plays that were heavily influenced by Greek tragedy and often based on Greek mythology. Unusually for the time, many featured women in the title role. Another great dramatist of the era, Molière (1622–73), developed French comedy with plays that mocked the middle classes.

Spain

The 17th century was the Golden Age of Spanish theatre. The Spanish dramatist Lope de Vega (1562–1635) wrote some 1,500 plays; his play *Fuenteovejuna* was one of the first to deal with ordinary working people. The other great Spanish dramatist of this time was Pedro Calderón de la Barca (1600–81), who produced many tragedies and historical plays.

Types of drama

The many types of drama include tragedies (serious plays that deal with the downfall of a flawed but heroic individual) and light-hearted comedies (plays with happy endings). Other types include historical plays, thrillers, and musical theatre.

The stage is empty, except for a single tree.

The heroes wait for someone who does not arrive.

Waiting for Godot (1955), by Irish writer Samuel Beckett (1906–89), is a type of modern drama known as the "Theatre of the Absurd": the plot seems to lead nowhere, suggesting life has no point.

Realism and 20th century

From the mid-18th century onwards, drama became increasingly realistic, with playwrights portraying middle-class characters in familiar situations. Theatres were fitted with picture-frame stages and realistic sets. It was fashionable for plays to deliver a direct, moral message. During the 20th century, dramatists experimented with dialogue and plot structure, in order to challenge "realism" or give dramas a symbolic meaning.

A Doll's House **(1879), by Ibsen**

Realistic drama

Dramatists such as Norwegian Henrik Ibsen (1828–1906) and Swede August Strindberg (1849–1912) produced plays that attacked the narrow social attitudes of their time and sometimes shocked audiences with their frankness.

Mother Courage **(1941), by Brecht, is set during the Thirty Years' War.**

Bertolt Brecht

In his plays, the German writer Bertolt Brecht (1898–1956) put forward serious socialist messages. He constantly reminded his audience that they were watching a play, to make them think about the socialist ideas in his works, and look more closely at the world outside the theatre.

Broadway

A street in New York at the heart of the city's theatre-going district, Broadway is world famous, and synonymous with the commercial theatre in North America. Broadway productions need a big budget and guaranteed audiences, so more experimental plays often appear in theatres "off-Broadway" first, and transfer to a Broadway theatre if successful.

Broadcasting

Anyone with access to a television or radio can now enjoy drama every day. Sometimes these are productions of works originally written for the stage, and adapted. More common are dramas specially written for broadcasting. Many of these are run as series, so that every week, or even every day, people can watch or listen to another episode of their favourite drama. Some forms of television drama have proved especially popular, such as crime stories, adventure series, and soap operas.

O Maraja, *satirical Brazilian soap opera*

Soap operas
Immensely popular, these serialized television dramas usually deal with the lives and loves of "ordinary" people. Soap operas are so-called because they were at first sponsored by commercial companies such as soap manufacturers.

Actors

The skill of the actors is vital to the success of a drama. Using the right tone of voice, facial expression, or gesture, an actor creates the illusion that the audience is watching or listening to real people and events on stage or screen. Many actors study at drama school before becoming professionals, paid to appear on stage.

D

Chinese opera
Traditional Chinese, or Beijing, opera retells stories from historical events and Buddhist stories. The action comprises arias and recitations, mime, song, and dance, with music from an orchestra of traditional instruments, such as the lute, clappers, gongs, and drums.

Farewell My Concubine is a film about Chinese opera.

World drama

Many non-Western cultures have produced their own, distinct traditions of drama, which draw on local conditions and skills. In Asia, for example, drama draws on local mythology and tales of gods and goddesses. Such drama also uses local craft skills to produce striking costumes and masks, and may be accompanied with music played on traditional instruments.

At a festival held each year in Salzburg, Austria, actors re-enact a medieval religious drama.

Drama festivals
Drama festivals are held around the world so that theatre-goers can celebrate the best in acting and writing. Plays range from traditional productions to experimental works from new writers. The Edinburgh International Festival, held annually, is world famous.

Noh theatre
In traditional Japanese Noh drama, actors wear elaborate costumes and masks, but perform on a bare stage. They move slowly and make special, meaningful gestures. They chant their lines, accompanied by music. Plays are performed in groups, the whole programme lasting an entire day.

Noh mask

Noh masks represent five groups: male, female, old people, the gods, and monsters.

Ritual drama
In parts of Africa, Asia, and Melanesia, traditional drama forms an important part of religious ritual. A high priest or shaman puts on a mask and costume that completely disguises him and, as he dances to music, people believe that he actually becomes the spirit he is imitating.

Papua New Guinea Trobrianders: ritual religious drama.

Circuses
A circus is a form of entertainment that combines a number of different skills, such as juggling, acrobatics, clowning, and conjuring. Circuses date from the end of the 18th century. Animal acts once formed part of circus routines, but these are now less popular in the West.

Moscow State Circus

Javanese shadow puppet

In shadow plays, puppets are used to tell traditional stories.

Made from leather

The operator uses thin rods to move the puppet.

Puppetry

Puppetry is a type of drama involving puppets, figures that seem to come to life when a human operator moves them. It is one of the oldest types of drama, dating from at least the 5th century BC. One example is shadow puppetry, which is popular in Southeast Asia. A light is used to cast a shadow from the puppet onto a translucent viewing screen. The puppet then acts out a play.

Robert Lepage

The Canadian playwright and director Robert Lepage (b. 1957) has achieved world status for his experimental work. Giving everyday objects symbolic meaning, and working closely with actors, he has taken risks that, while not always a critical success, push back the boundaries of drama.

Timeline

5th century BC The Greeks pioneer tragedy and comedy.

11th to 15th centuries AD Religious drama becomes popular in Europe.

Statue of comic actor from Roman drama

1580–1642 In England, the Elizabethan and Jacobean dramatists revitalize English drama.

1600–80 The Golden Age of Spanish drama.

1782 Friedrich von Schiller (1759–1805) stages *The Robbers*, one of the plays that inspires the German Romantic movement in the 18th century.

c.1800 In Vietnam, Hat Boi theatre dramatizes tales of war and suffering.

Late 1800s "Realist" drama develops, exploring modern social issues.

1960s The "Theatre of the Absurd" subverts the conventions of the theatre.

1990s Musicals are the most popular type of play.

FESTIVALS | FILMS AND FILM-MAKING | GREECE, ANCIENT | LITERATURE | MEDIEVAL EUROPE | OPERA | RENAISSANCE | SHAKESPEARE, WILLIAM | THEATRES

D

DRUGS

A DRUG IS ANY SUBSTANCE that, when put into the body, alters its normal workings or body chemistry. Natural body hormones, such as insulin, can act as drugs when taken in concentrated form. Medical drugs have many uses. Some, such as cough suppressants, may relieve symptoms; others, such as analgesics, deaden pain; while others, including antibiotics, treat the cause of disease. Drugs may also be taken for non-medical reasons, such as steroids to enhance sports performance and body-building. The abuse of such drugs may be illegal, and can cause physical harm.

Pestle

Mortar

History of drugs

More than 3,000 years ago, people across the world – especially in China, India, the Middle East, Europe, and North Africa – used hundreds of different substances as drugs. They included herbal and mineral extracts, and animal products, such as blood, bile, and urine. Physicians mixed these drugs using a pestle and mortar, and often combined their use with magic, superstition, and religion. Modern research has discovered that some are effective.

Types of drugs

Drugs can be grouped by their medical uses or effects. For example, antibiotics kill bacteria, analgesics deaden pain, anti-inflammatories reduce swelling, anti-pyretics lower body temperature, and anti-coagulants help to prevent unwanted blood clots. Some drugs, such as aspirin, can be placed in more than one category.

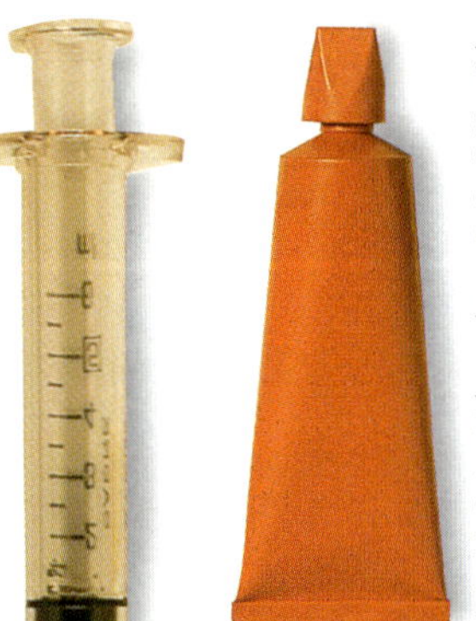

Antibiotic

These drugs kill or disable germs (harmful microbes) known as bacteria. Most come from chemicals made either by fungi, or by other bacteria.

Antibiotic cream

Analgesic

Painkillers come in two types: narcotics, such as morphine, codeine, and other opiates originally from the opium poppy; and non-narcotics, such as paracetamol, which have a different origin.

Cytotoxic

The name means "cell-poisoners", but cytotoxic drugs are designed to affect only the out-of-control cells in tumours and malignancies (cancers), while leaving normal body cells unharmed. They are one type of anti-cancer drug. They are very powerful and their doses and uses must be carefully supervised.

Syringe containing cytotoxic drugs

Tablets and capsules

How drugs work

Drugs change the processes within the cells of the body. Their effectiveness depends on the dose (quantity), and method of administration (or route into the body). These routes include: absorption through the skin from a cream or a skin patch; injections into a muscle, vein, or under the skin; inhalation; eye or ear drops; or the oral route, where medication is swallowed as tablets, pills, capsules, or liquid.

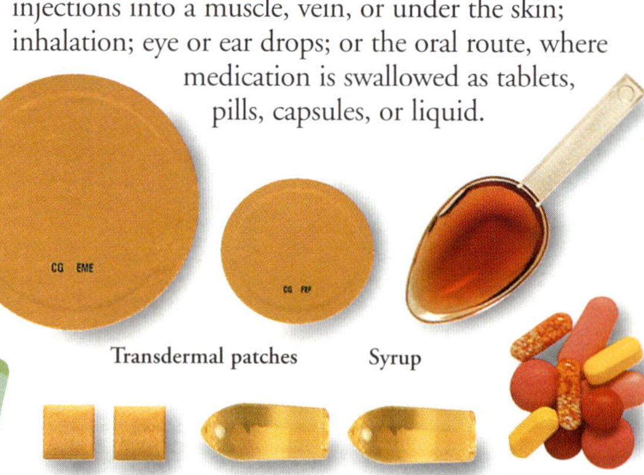

Pressurized inhaler

Transdermal patches

Syrup

Chewing gum

Suppositories

Pills and tablets

Drugs from nature

Half of modern drugs originate from plants, fungi, animals, or microbes. In ancient times, people were unable to separate the actual drug – the active ingredient – from its source. As chemistry became more sophisticated, scientists identified and purified these ingredients making the drug safer. Some drugs extracted originally from nature are now made from genetically engineered microbes.

Fresh leaves

Witch hazel

Resin

Dried parts

Paul Ehrlich

The German scientist Paul Ehrlich (1854–1915) dreamed of finding a substance that would act as a "magic bullet", by destroying invading germs, while leaving healthy body cells unaffected. He pioneered synthetic drugs (chemical agents made in the laboratory, rather than extracted from natural sources). The first of these was Salvarsan, which was a laboratory-made drug containing arsenic; it was effective against syphilis and related infections.

Drug research laboratory

Drug research

In the laboratory, scientists analyse potential new drugs. They perform tests on the drug to establish its chemistry, and how it affects the body's processes. Then they test it on tissues and cells in the laboratory, on animals, and finally on human volunteers in clinical trials.

Aspirin

Brand name – the name by which manufacturers sell a drug, e.g. Aspro.

Generic name – the name by which the active ingredient is known, e.g. aspirin.

Common chemical name – showing the chemical subgroups, e.g. acetyl-salicylic acid.

Chemical formula – lists the atoms and their numbers in the drug, e.g. $C_9H_8O_4$.

Pharmacies

The science of drugs is known as pharmacology. Pharmacy refers to both the practice of preparing and dispensing drugs, and the place where this happens. A person qualified in pharmacology is called a pharmacist (or chemist). The dispensing chemist can advise on which drugs to use for minor ailments.

Pharmacist at work

Prescription

Some drugs, known as controlled substances, are only available with a doctor's permission. A prescription is a written and signed instruction from a doctor that authorizes a pharmacist to dispense a controlled substance. Prescriptions include the name and dosage of the drug, how often the patient must take it, and any other relevant instructions.

Hospital pharmacy

Over-the-counter drugs

Over-the-counter drugs are available without a prescription. They can be bought at supermarkets and pharmacies, and are usually less powerful than prescription drugs. They have fewer side-effects or contra-indications (health problems that warn against their use), but they are still open to misuse. Pharmacists are qualified to recommend certain drug preparations, although they cannot diagnose or prescribe treatment.

Non-medical drugs

Some drugs can be taken for their non-medicinal effects on the mind and body. These effects may include the stimulation or sedation of the mind, a temporary boost to physical performance in sport, or a feeling of emotional well-being.

Wine and brandy

Sedatives

These drugs sedate (slow down) bodily functions, including physical activity and mental agility. Sedatives can make the user feel relaxed and peaceful for a short time. They include sleeping pills, antihistamines (which suppress allergic reactions), antidepressants, and alcohol, which is probably the most widely used non-medical drug in the world.

Caffeine is found in coffee, tea, and cola.

Coffee

Stimulants

These drugs temporarily stimulate (speed up) bodily functions and mental processes. However, they can cause after-effects, such as depression. Stimulants include caffeine, nicotine (in tobacco), and cocaine.

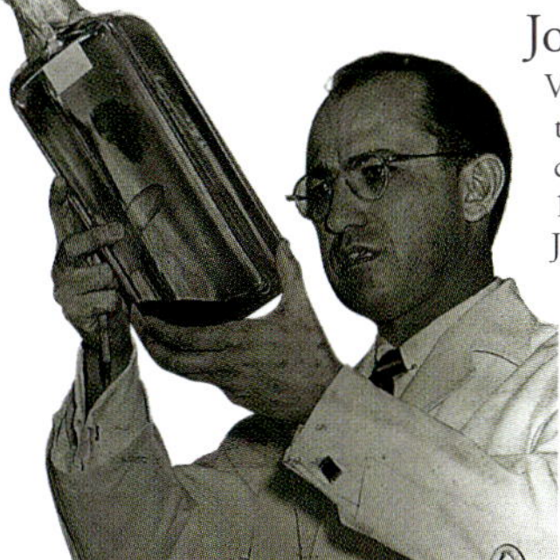

Jonas Salk

Vaccines are substances that give the body resistance or immunity to certain infecting germs. In the 1950s, American microbiologist Jonas Salk (1914–95) developed the first effective vaccine against the crippling disease of polio (poliomyelitis). It spread into worldwide use from 1955 on. From 1960, an oral form of the vaccine, Sabin, gradually replaced the Salk injection.

Drug abuse

This is the improper non-medical use of legal or illegal drugs for physical or psychological reasons. The feelings and mental state experienced by the taker are often very different to that person's actual behaviour, seen by onlookers. After too much alcohol, a drinker may feel bright and witty, while onlookers see a slurring bore.

Tobacco shop

Customs official arresting a drug trafficker

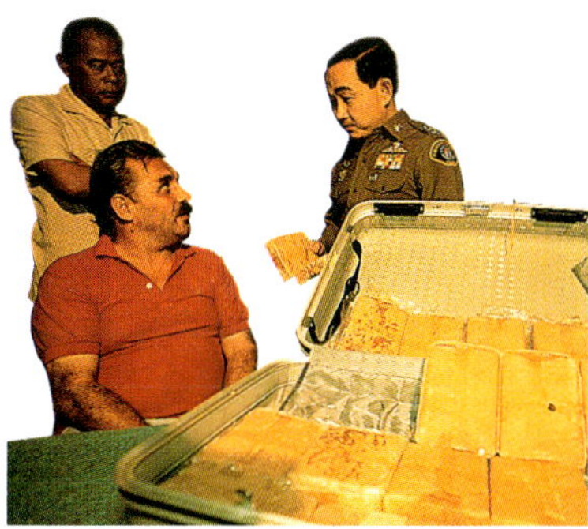

Illegal drugs

Some drugs are so powerful and dangerous that they are illegal almost everywhere in the world. These include LSD and mescaline (known in some countries as Schedule I drugs), amphetamines, cocaine, and narcotics (Schedule II drugs). Supplying these illegal drugs to users has become a vast international business.

Legal drugs

The legality of drugs varies greatly all over the world. As well as the drug's strength and effects, legality often depends on tradition, religion, and availability. One of the most powerful and addictive drugs is alcohol. Alcohol is fully legalized in some countries, partly legalized (for people over 18 or 21) in others, and completely banned in others. Nicotine in the form of cigars, cigarettes, chewing tobacco, and snuff is also legal in most countries.

Group therapy session

Dependence and addiction

A person may come to depend on addictive drugs in order to function. Addiction – intense craving – is hard to control. If the user stops taking the drug, his or her body undergoes "withdrawal", which includes symptoms, such as headaches, sweating, hallucinations, and mood swings. People trying to stop using addictive drugs often find support groups are helpful.

Timeline

1840s Anaesthetics begin to be used during surgery.

1881 Artificial vaccine used against anthrax.

1910 Paul Ehrlich introduces chemo-therapeutic drugs.

1922 Frederick Banting and others treat diabetes using insulin, a natural body hormone.

1936 Treatment of infections improves with the advent of Prontosil, the first sulpha drug.

Fresh witch hazel

1940s Howard Florey and Ernst Chain make penicillin available as an antibiotic. It is used widely in World War II.

1956 Oral contraceptives (birth control pills) are introduced, using the natural female hormones, oestrogen and progestogen.

1967 Fertility drugs help couples conceive.

1983 Cyclosporin, an immuno-suppressant, helps prevent rejection of transplanted organs.

1990s AIDS drugs tested.

Tablets and capsules

FIND OUT MORE
FIRST AID · HOSPITALS · MEDICINE · MEDICINE, HISTORY OF · PASTEUR, LOUIS · PLANT USES

DUCKS, GEESE, AND SWANS

MOST DUCKS, GEESE, AND SWANS spend their life on or near water. They belong to a family of birds called waterfowl and are closely related to each other. They have broad beaks and short legs with webbed feet. They are good swimmers and have waterproof plumage, which keeps them dry and also helps them to float. There are about 160 species of waterfowl in the wild. Some species of duck and goose have been domesticated and are often raised on farms.

Khaki Campbell – a domestic duck

Ducks

Ducks are the smallest and most varied waterfowl. Males are often brightly coloured and females are usually drab, which helps to camouflage them when they are sitting on their eggs. Some ducks live in coastal waters, but most live on rivers, lakes, and ponds.

Webs stretched open

Webs closed

Swimming

A duck's webbed feet work like paddles to push it through the water. When it pushes its feet backward, it spreads its toes to stretch out the webs between them. When it pulls its feet forward, it closes its toes to shut the webs, which then offer less water resistance.

Plumage

Ducks produce a waterproof oil from a gland near the base of their tail. When they preen their feathers, they spread the oil over them. This oil is so effective that a duck stays dry even when it dives beneath the surface.

Swans

The largest waterfowl are swans, with a wingspan of up to 2.3 m (7.5 ft). Most of the eight species are white, but the Australian black swan has a black body and white flight feathers. A swan spends a lot of its time on water. It uses its long neck to reach plants below the surface.

Mute swan has a black knob at the base of its beak.

Mute swan egg is an oval shape.

Swan egg

Young swans

Young swans, or cygnets, stay with their parents for a whole year, which is a long time for a bird. When they develop their adult plumage, their parents drive them away.

Nesting swans

Swans nest on the ground close to the water's edge. The female incubates the eggs for up to 38 days, and she hisses loudly at anything that comes too close. If her warnings are ignored, she attacks. Her powerful beak and wings make formidable weapons.

A Mandarin duckling leaves the nest in response to its mother's call.

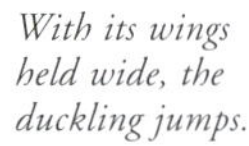

With its wings held wide, the duckling jumps.

Big feet and stubby wings work like parachutes to slow the duckling's fall.

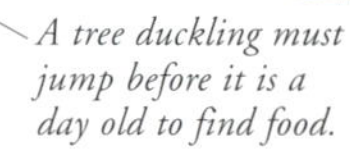

A tree duckling must jump before it is a day old to find food.

Tree-nesting ducks

Most ducks nest on the ground but a few lay their eggs in holes in trees. Soon after the young have hatched, their mother leaves the nest and calls to them to follow her. The ducklings are too young to fly, and instead they jump to the ground.

The duckling walks away on landing.

Geese

Unlike most waterfowl, geese usually feed on land. They eat grass, gripping it in their beaks and pulling it up with a tug. Many geese breed in the tundra of the far north. These white-fronted geese, seen here in western Scotland, fly north to Greenland after the winter.

Swan takeoff

Swans can weigh up to 13 kg (28.5 lb), which makes them among the world's heaviest flying birds. Swans cannot take off from a standing start. Instead, they have to run across the water to gain enough speed for takeoff.

MUTE SWAN

SCIENTIFIC NAME	*Cygnus olor*
ORDER	Anseriformes
FAMILY	Anatidae
DISTRIBUTION	Western Europe, parts of central Asia; also introduced into other parts of the world, including North America, Australia, and New Zealand
HABITAT	Lakes and rivers
DIET	Water plants
SIZE	Length: 152 cm (60 in)
LIFESPAN	About 20 years

FIND OUT MORE: ANIMAL BEHAVIOUR · BIRDS · EGGS · FARMING · FLIGHT, ANIMAL · PENGUINS · SEABIRDS

DYES AND PAINTS

DYES AND PAINTS are substances that are used to stain or give colour to a range of objects, from textiles and paper to buildings and machinery. The substances that give colour to dyes are called dyestuffs, which, when dissolved in water, penetrate the fibres of fabrics by means of a chemical reaction. Pigments form the colour in paints. These are held in place using a varnish-like substance called a vehicle, or binder, which also binds the pigment to the surface being painted. Throughout history, people have created colour, first by means of natural dyes and pigments, and today by using synthetic ones.

Early pigments

The first materials used as pigments were probably coloured clays, which were mixed with water or animal oils to make paint. Dyes made from plants and animals were later used to colour textiles. Common plant dyes included woad, madder, saffron, and turmeric. Animal sources included cochineal (beetle) and the Murex sea snail.

Red skin of onion gives colour

Stinging nettle

Walnuts

Turmeric leaf

Root

Powder

Turmeric

Saffron powder

Saffron crocus

Dyes

Some natural dyes still exist, but most used today are synthetic. These are organic chemicals produced by processing petroleum and coal-tar chemicals such as benzene. Most dyes are used in the textile industry, but are also used in the leather, paper, food, and cosmetics industries. The dyes can be applied to the fibre or fabric using either a direct or indirect process.

Wool can by dyed using a mordant dye, but this dye is now avoided in Western countries due to its use of potentially harmful chemicals.

Indirect dyeing

In some dyeing processes, a number of steps are needed to dye the fibre. In one process, a chemical called a mordant is first added to the fibre, which is then dyed. The mordant molecules fix the dye to the fabric.

Fabrics can be coloured using a range of dyes

Direct dyeing

In most industrial dyeing processes today, dyes can enter the fibre and colour it in one step, without the need of a mordant. The dye is dissolved in hot water, strained, and then added to the fabric. Sometimes the dye is mixed with salt to help fix the colour.

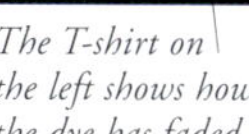

The T-shirt on the left shows how the dye has faded.

This T-shirt shows how the colour has remained fast.

Colour fastness

Two of the most important properties demanded of a dye by clothes manufacturers are its abilities to resist being washed out, and not to fade in the light. The colour fastness of a fabric also varies according to the dyeing process that is used and the type of material that is being dyed.

Paints

Paint comes in many colours and can be used as a coating on rigid structures such as houses, bridges, ships, and cars. Finer paints are used by artists to produce imaginative and colourful works of art. The pigments used to make the paints may be natural, such as rutile (titanium dioxide) or synthetic, such as phthalocyanine blue.

Industrial paints

Industrial paints are custom-made for specific jobs. Some paints contain powdered metal and metal oxides, so that the paint can protect exposed structures, such as iron bridges. Paints such as those used on cars are designed to withstand rusting and high temperatures.

Oil paints usually come in tubes so that users can squeeze out the exact amount of paint needed.

Oil paints

Artists' paints

Artists use a variety of types of paint to achieve different effects, including watercolours, oils, and acrylics. The pigments in watercolour paints are mixed with a water solution of gum arabic, in oils they are mixed in a slow-drying oil, such as linseed oil, while in acrylics the pigments are mixed with a synthetic-resin vehicle.

Paint-spraying car body

Domestic paints

Most decorating paints are made for easy application. Non-drip paints are jelly-like in the can, but flow easily when applied. Emulsion paint uses water as its vehicle, so splashes can be removed and brushes easily cleaned.

Can of non-drip paint and brush

William Henry Perkin

British chemist William Henry Perkin (1838–1907) accidentally produced the first synthetic dye, mauve, in 1856. He was attempting to make the drug quinine from coal-tar chemicals, but instead produced a purple liquid dye. This was the start of the synthetic dye industry.

FIND OUT MORE

ART, HISTORY OF · CHEMISTRY · CLOTHES AND FASHION · COAL · COLOUR · MIXTURES AND COMPOUNDS · MONET, CLAUDE · PAINTING AND DRAWING · TEXTILES AND WEAVING

EARS AND HEARING

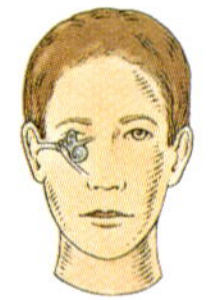

When a bee buzzes, a soprano sings, or a jumbo jet takes off, each generates invisible vibrations called sound waves that enter the ears, the body's organs of hearing. The sound waves travel deep inside the skull to the part of the ear that does the hearing. Here, sound waves are converted into nerve impulses that travel along nerves to the auditory, or hearing, area on each side of the brain. In the brain, the impulses are interpreted as sounds. The ears can pick up a wide range of sounds and, with the eyes, they help us to make sense of our surroundings.

Anatomy of the ear

Mostly concealed within the skull, the ear is divided into three parts. The outer ear consists of the pinna (ear flap) and the auditory canal. The middle ear is filled with air and contains three tiny bones called ossicles. The inner ear is fluid-filled and contains the cochlea and the semicircular canals.

Temporal bone

Semicircular canal

Inner ear

Cochlea

Middle ear contains three bones called the ossicles: the malleus, incus, and stapes.

Eardrum

Auditory canal carries sound into ear and produces wax that keeps the ear dust and insect free.

Eustachian tube connects middle ear to throat to equalize air pressure inside and outside the ear.

Pinna

Hearing sounds

Sound waves channelled into the auditory canal cause the eardrum and the ossicles to vibrate. These vibrations travel through the fluid-filled cochlea. Inside the cochlea, sensory hair cells convert the vibrations into nerve impulses. These are carried by the cochlear nerve to the brain.

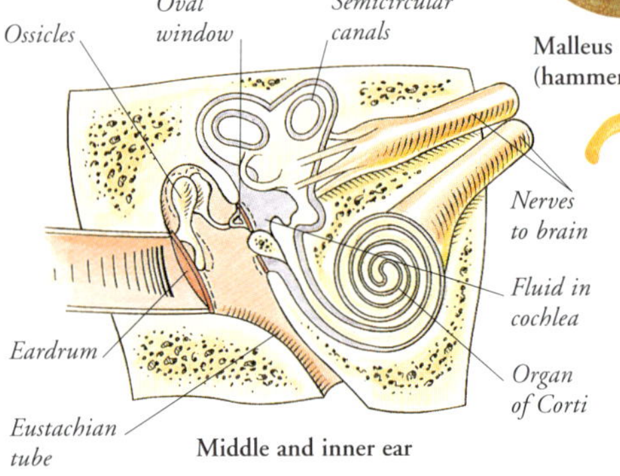

Middle and inner ear

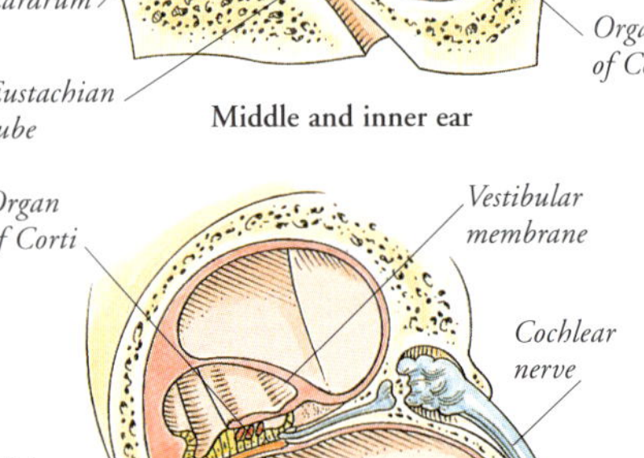

This cutaway of the cochlea shows its 3 chambers.

Cochlea

The cochlea is a long, coiled tube in the inner ear that is filled with fluid. It is divided by two membranes into three chambers that run lengthways. The middle of these three chambers, the cochlear chamber, contains the spiral organ of Corti, which consists of over 20,000 sensory hair cells that send nerve signals to the brain.

Eardrum

The eardrum, or tympanic membrane, is a taut piece of skin that separates the auditory canal from the middle ear. When sound waves hit the eardrum, it vibrates like a drum and transmits its vibrations to the ossicles of the middle ear.

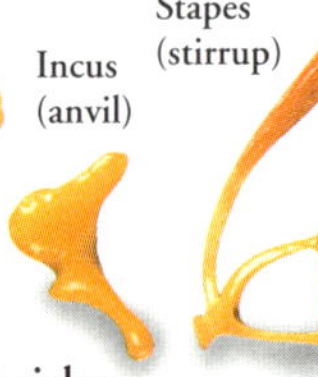

Malleus (hammer)

Incus (anvil)

Stapes (stirrup)

Ossicles

The ossicles are the three smallest bones in the body. The malleus, incus, and stapes connect the eardrum to the cochlea by way of the oval window.

Bartolomeo Eustachio

Italian anatomist Bartolomeo Eustachio (1520–74) studied the detailed anatomy of the ear, as well as other body organs and systems, while he was a professor in Rome. He wrote the first full description of the ears in his book *The Examination of the Organ of Hearing*, published in 1562. Included in this was the first detailed description of the tube that links the middle ear with the throat. This was later named the Eustachian tube.

Air pressure

You hear most clearly when the air pressure inside the middle ear is the same as the air pressure outside your body. If the air pressure outside changes suddenly, you may not be able to hear properly. This can happen if you are a on a plane that is taking off or landing, or if you are travelling on a fast train.

Balance

Part of the inner ear helps you to balance. Sensors inside the three semicircular canals detect movements made by the head and the rest of the body. Sensors inside two adjoining chambers, the saccule and utricle, detect whether the body is upright, upside-down, or in between. Nerve impulses from the semicircular canals are analysed by the brain to assess the body's position.

Gymnast's outstretched arms help balance.

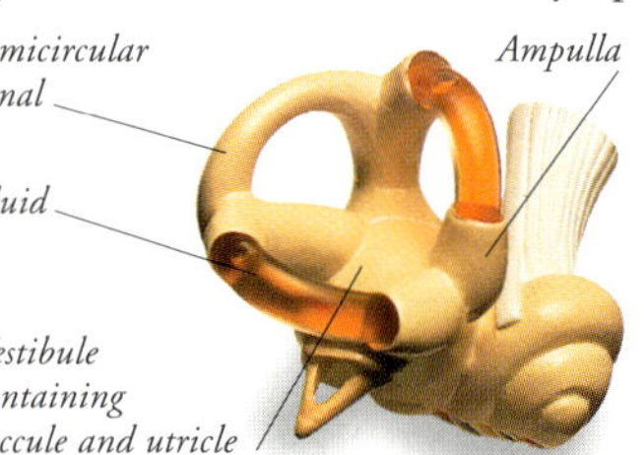

Semicircular canals

The three semicircular canals in each ear are filled with fluid. At the base of each canal is a bulge, called an ampulla, which contains sensory hair cells that send impulses to the brain. The three canals are set at 90° to each other, so they can detect movement in any direction.

Hearing ranges

The pitch of a sound depends on the frequency of the sound waves that produced it. High-pitched sounds have a high frequency, and low-pitched sounds have a low frequency. Frequency is measured in units called Hertz (Hz). Our hearing ability decreases as we get older, from 20,000 to 12,000 Hz.

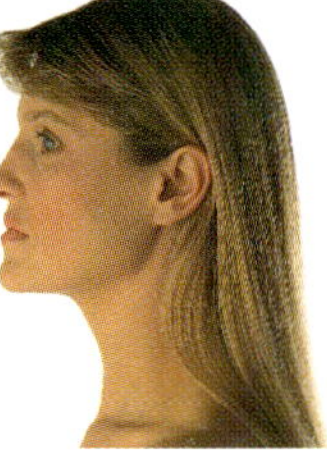

20–20,000 Hz

Bats' ears can hear very high-pitched sound waves called ultrasound.

1,000–120,000 Hz

FIND OUT MORE
BRAIN AND NERVOUS SYSTEM
HUMAN BODY
MUSIC
SOUND

EARTH

WE LIVE ON A GIANT BALL OF ROCK spinning round the Sun, which we call the Earth. The Earth is one of nine planets in the Solar System and one of the four made of rock. However, the Earth is unique, because it is the only planet in the Solar System – and perhaps even in the Universe – that can support life. The distance of the Earth from the Sun makes it neither very hot like Venus, nor icy cold like Pluto, enabling liquid water to exist on its surface. The Earth also has an oxygen-rich atmosphere. These two substances – water and oxygen – are the key factors that allow life to flourish on the Earth.

Structure of the Earth

By recording the way vibrations from earthquakes reverberate through the Earth, scientists have discovered that the Earth has an egg-like structure. At its centre is a "yolk" of metal, surrounded by an "egg-white" of soft rock called the mantle, and an outer "shell" of hard rock called the crust.

The Earth's crust consists of a number of interlocking slabs of rock called tectonic plates.

Earth's ingredients

Although more than 80 elements (basic substances) occur naturally on the Earth, the bulk of the Earth is made of iron (35%), oxygen (28%), magnesium (17%), and silicon (13%). The following elements are present in significant, but small, amounts: nickel (2.7%), sulphur (2.7%), calcium (0.6%), and aluminium (0.6%). Tiny proportions of other elements make up the remainder (0.6%).

Solid iron

Molecule of oxygen gas

Magnesium ore (magnesite)

Locket containing crystal of silicon

Nickel ore (nickeline)

Sulphur crystals

Investigating Earth's composition

By taking rock samples from the Earth's interior, geologists have been able to understand the Earth's chemical make-up. Analysis of meteorites – solid pieces from an exploded planet – has led some geologists to believe that the Earth may have formed from the same space debris of which meteorites are made.

Chondrite meteorite

Meteorites

Meteorites are natural objects that fall to the Earth from space. They are made of iron, stone, or a mixture of both. The two main types of meteorite are called chondrites and achondrites.

Calcium-rich chalk

Aluminium ore (bauxite)

Achondrite meteorite

The Earth's structure

Atmosphere is a thin surrounding layer of gases about 640 km (400 miles) deep.

Crust, Earth's outer layer of rock varies in thickness: beneath the oceans, it is 6–11 km (4–7 miles) thick, but it stretches up to 70 km (43 miles) under mountain ranges.

Mohorovicic discontinuity, or Moho, is the boundary between the crust and the mantle.

Mantle is a partially molten layer beneath the crust, extending to a depth of about 2,900 km (1,800 miles) and made largely of a rock called peridotite.

Gutenberg discontinuity is the boundary between the mantle and the core.

Outer core reaches to a depth of about 4,900 km (3,050 miles) and is made of molten iron and nickel – magnetic metals that give the Earth its magnetic field.

Inner core, like the outer core, is made of iron and nickel, but although temperatures reach 3,700°C (6,690°F), the pressure is so great that the metal remains solid.

Richard Oldham

By examining the seismographic recordings of earthquakes, the British geologist Richard Oldham (1858–1936) discovered that earthquakes produce two different kinds of vibration. He called them primary (P) waves and secondary (S) waves. Oldham's analysis revealed that P waves travel more slowly through the core of the Earth than through the mantle. He concluded that Earth's core must be liquid, which is partly true.

E

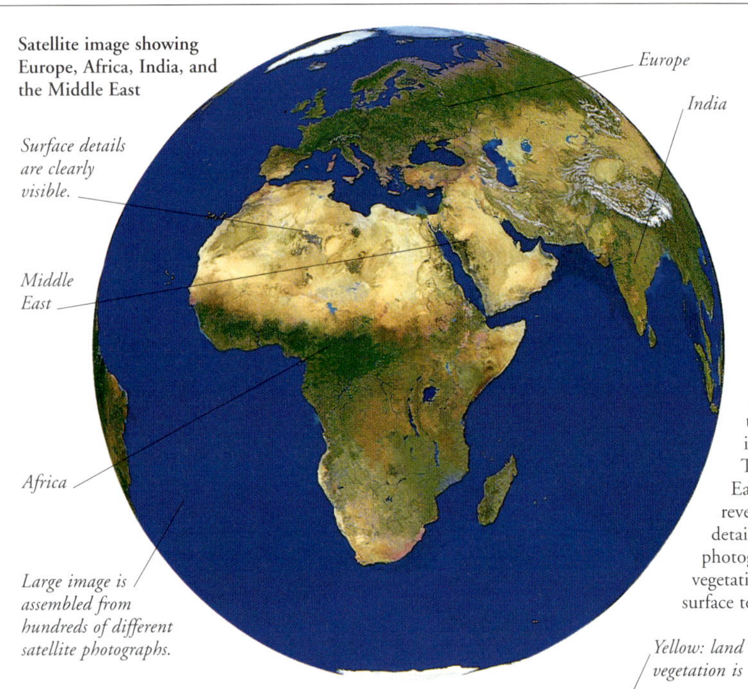

Satellite image showing Europe, Africa, India, and the Middle East

Surface details are clearly visible.

Middle East

Africa

Large image is assembled from hundreds of different satellite photographs.

Earth system

Planet Earth seems to operate like a vast, complex system made up of various interconnected processes that keep conditions stable and suitable for life. The atmosphere's unique make up, for example, ensures that the Earth stays at an ideal temperature for life, never heating up or cooling down by more than a few degrees. Scientists now realize that the environment must be treated with care, because a change to one part of this complex system may have unpredictable repercussions in other parts.

Earth from space

Much of what scientists know about the interrelated parts of the Earth system comes from images sent back by satellites. These images show us that the Earth is roughly spherical and reveal surface features in clear detail. Special heat-sensitive infrared photographs show the distribution of vegetation and variations in the Earth's surface temperature.

Energy regulation

The Earth system exchanges energy with its surroundings, but there is no overall gain or loss of energy. The Earth receives heat, light, and other forms of energy directly from the Sun. Some of this energy is reflected back by the clouds, oceans, land, and atmosphere; the rest is absorbed and then released back into space. The total energy the Earth gives out equals the total energy it receives from the Sun.

Infrared image of temperature variations in the Atlantic Ocean off the USA's eastern coast

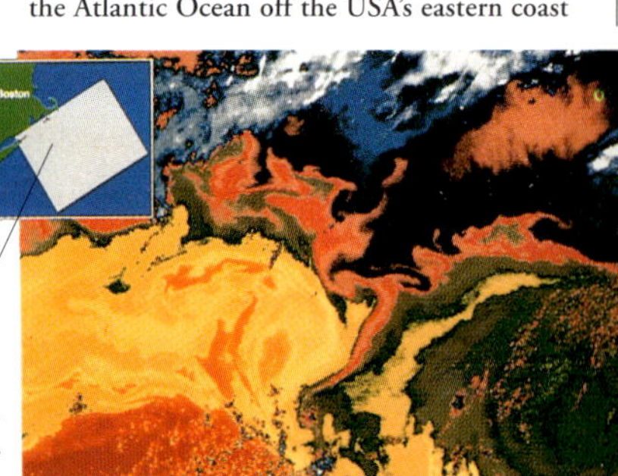

Locator map

Biosphere

Between the atmosphere's lowest layers and the ocean floor is a rich diversity of life, from tiny ocean organisms called plankton to the largest trees and animals. Together, these organisms form the biosphere – the living part of the planet. Satellite images can help scientists understand the complicated links between living things and the Earth.

Green: land areas where vegetation is most dense

Yellow: land areas where vegetation is least dense

Red: ocean areas where plankton is most dense

Blue: ocean areas where plankton is least dense

Infrared image of vegetation and plankton distribution

Gaia theory

British scientist James Lovelock (b. 1919) suggests that the Earth and all the lifeforms upon it function as if they were a single living organism. He calls this "organism" Gaia, after the Greek goddess of fertility. Like any other organism, he says, Gaia is self-regulating, meaning that it will naturally change its environment to maintain the right conditions for life – even if humans make the Earth unfit for themselves by polluting it and using up its limited resources.

Greek statue of Gaia, 450 BC

Theories about the Earth

There have been many theories about the Earth that may seem strange to people today, but which were widely believed at the time. The ancient Egyptians, for example, thought that the Earth was a flat square under a pyramid-shaped sky, and people in medieval Europe believed that it was the Sun that revolved around the Earth, and not vice versa. Similarly, before technology enabled scientists to understand more about the interior of the Earth, people suggested that the Earth was hollow.

Hollow Earth theory

People assumed the Earth had a vast, empty core.

Hidden lands and oceans, complete with plants and animals and warmed by a subterranean Sun, were thought to lie within the centre of the Earth.

Search for another Earth

Astronomers have recently detected signs of the existence of planets beyond the Solar System. Wobbles in the movements of the stars 47 Ursae Majoris, 70 Virginis, and 51 Pegasi suggest that they may be orbited by planets – perhaps even ones similar to the Earth. Astronomers have found other stars with solar systems forming around them.

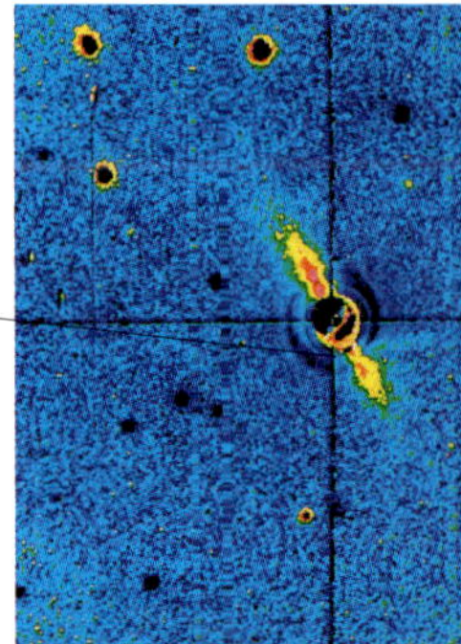

The yellow-and-red area may be another solar system forming around Beta Pictoris.

False-colour satellite image of the star Beta Pictoris, about 50 light years away

Timeline

c.4,600 mya The Earth and the other planets form as parts of a vast cloud of hot gas and dust circling the Sun begin to cluster together.

c.4,300 mya The Earth's crust forms.

c.4,200 mya As the Earth cools, gas bubbles and water vapour rise from the interior to form a cloudy atmosphere.

Gneiss rock

c.4,000 mya The crust and mantle separate; rain begins to fall; the atmosphere clears.

c.3,800 mya The first organisms are single-celled bacteria.

c.3,000 mya The atmosphere becomes oxygen-rich as ocean plants absorb sunlight and release oxygen into the air.

c.1,500 mya Protists, such as amoeba, are the first complex living cells; later, protists join up to form sponges – the first multi-celled organisms.

Sponge

c.570 mya A huge variety of complex lifeforms develops in the Earth's seas and oceans.

c.440–400 mya Land-based plants and animals become widespread.

c.220 mya There is a single, vast land mass, now known as Pangaea, which later breaks up into the smaller land masses we today call continents.

c.200–70 mya The era of the dinosaurs.

c.100,000 ya First modern humans appear.

ATMOSPHERE · CONTINENTS · EARTH SCIENCES · ELEMENTS · FOSSILS · GEOLOGY · MAGNETISM · PLANETS · SUN AND SOLAR SYSTEM

EARTHQUAKES

FROM A GENTLE RIPPLE to terrifying and violent movements in the Earth, earthquakes literally rock the world. Earthquakes are tremors in the ground, created by the sudden movement of tectonic plates – huge slabs of rock that make up the Earth's crust. The majority of earthquakes are so gentle that no one notices them, but some are so violent they destroy whole cities. An earthquake's effect and intensity are measured on different scales. In earthquake-prone countries, planning minimizes the damage earthquakes cause.

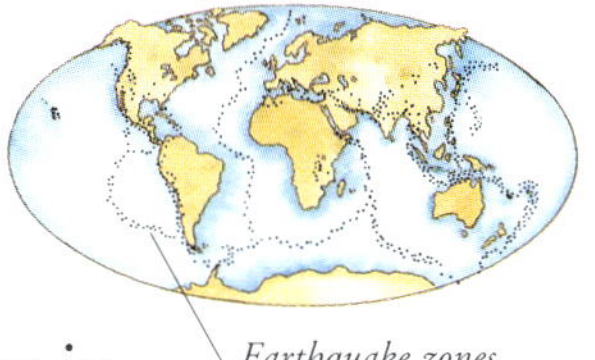

Earthquake zones

Earthquake zones
Although earthquakes can occur anywhere, they are more frequent in earthquake zones. These zones, such as Japan and California, lie near the moving margins of the tectonic plates, called fault lines.

What is an earthquake?

Tectonic plates usually slide past each other, but sometimes they get stuck together. The stress on the rocks builds up until they fault (crack). The tectonic plates then jolt past each other, sending shock waves through the ground. These vibrations, known as seismic waves, cause the earth to quake.

Epicentre
The point at which an earthquake occurs is known as the focus. Above the focus is the epicentre – the point on the Earth's surface where the effects of an earthquake are most devastating. The focus may be as much as 700 km (185 miles) below the epicentre. In 1985, an earthquake in Mexico City, with its epicentre in the Pacific Ocean, left 9,500 people dead. It measured 8.1 on the Richter scale.

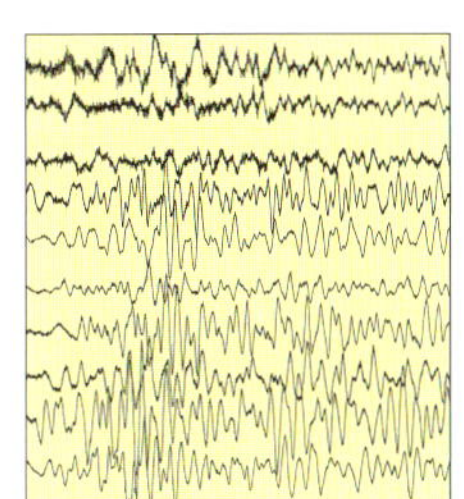

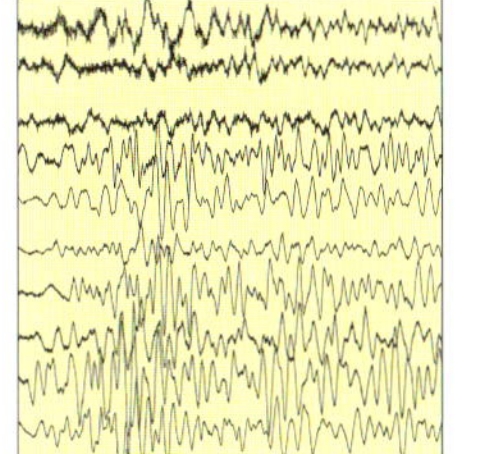

Seismometer
Seismometers show seismic waves, and measure an earthquake's location and intensity on the Richter scale. The height of each line shows the wave's force.

Reading from Kobe, Japan

aDestruction diminishes as shock waves travel away from the epicentre, recording less on the Richter scale.

Earthquake that causes small object to fall rates V on the Mercalli scale.

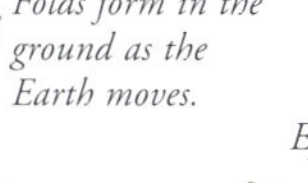

The Mercalli scale rates an earthquake according to its effect on a scale of I–XII: a swinging light bulb measures I; extensive structural damage measures XII.

Folds form in the ground as the Earth moves.

Epicentre

Focus

Shock waves radiate outwards in circles from focus.

The Richter scale measures the force of an earthquake on a scale from 1–10, taken from seismograph readings of the seismic waves. Each figure represents a force 10 times greater than that of the next lowest figure.

Tsunami

These are huge waves precipitated when an earthquake or volcanic eruption shakes the sea floor. Tsunamis roll along the ocean floor as fast as a jet plane. When they reach shallow coastal waters, they rear up into water ridges about 30 m (100 ft) high. Many tsunamis occur in the Pacific Ocean, such as the one in Hawaii, 1964 (left).

Earthquake proofing

Technology cannot prevent earthquakes but it can help limit their damage, particularly in building design. Most loss of life is caused not by the shaking ground, but by the collapse of buildings and roads, and fires started by damage to electrical equipment.

Building design
Pyramid-shaped, curved, and fire-resistant buildings and structures, such as this staircase in California, USA, bend rather than break during an earthquake. Mounting foundations on rubber also helps absorb some of the earthquake shocks.

Timeline

1556 Reports of an earthquake in the region of Shaanxi, China. Almost a million deaths.

1755 Lisbon, Portugal, is destroyed by an earthquake and the subsequent flood.

1883 Krakatoa Island destroyed by earthquake and tsunami.

1906 Quake flattens San Francisco, USA.

1964 Alaska hit by a very severe earthquake, measuring 9.2 on the Richter scale.

1964 Earthquake in Alaska generates a tsunami, which causes damage as far away as California, USA.

1976 Earthquake in China kills 255,000.

1990 In Iran 40,000 people die in quake.

1995 Kobe, central Japan, is devastated by an earthquake.

1999 Turkish quake kills 20,000 and makes 200,000 homeless.

2001 Earthquake in Gujarat, India, leaves 30,000 people dead.

FIND OUT MORE: BUILDING AND CONSTRUCTION · CONTINENTS · EARTH · GEOLOGY · OCEAN FLOOR · RADAR AND SONAR

EARTH SCIENCES

FOSSILS PROVIDE CLUES to the ages of rocks; the atmosphere provides clues to tomorrow's weather. Amongst others, these elements are studied within the discipline of Earth sciences. This is the study of the planet's physical characteristics, from volcanoes to raindrops. The different branches of Earth sciences cover all of the Earth's dynamic systems, apart from life forms, which are studied within biology. Knowledge about the Earth's history and formation also informs us about its needs, which will help ensure the future survival of the planet.

Branches of Earth sciences

The term Earth sciences has been used since the 1970s. It covers the range of subjects that were previously bracketed under the term "physical geography". Although each of the Earth sciences is a distinct study focusing on one aspect of the Earth, each is also a key element of the inter-related study of Earth sciences.

Pebbles

Anthracite, a form of coal

Granite

Geology

The oldest branch of the Earth sciences, geology is the study of the Earth's history, structure, and make-up. Although it centres on rocks and the composition of the Earth's crust, geology also relates to the other Earth sciences, except for meteorology.

Palaeontology

Fossils, the remains of once living organisms preserved in sedimentary rock, are studied within the branch of Earth science called palaeontology. From fossils, scientists can work out the ages of rocks and develop a picture of the history of plant and animal life on Earth over billions of years.

Fossil of a sea creature

Earth sciences cover many different areas of study.

Volcanology

The study of volcanoes, and the reasons why they erupt, is known as volcanology. It may involve volcanologists working close to an erupting volcano. The scientists wear special clothing to protect them from gas, heat, and flying lava bombs.

Volcanic bombs

Geomorphology

The study of landforms and the processes that shape them is known as geomorphology. It includes landforms ranging from mountains and valleys to rivers and glaciers, and the effects of different shaping processes upon them, such as the erosion caused by weathering.

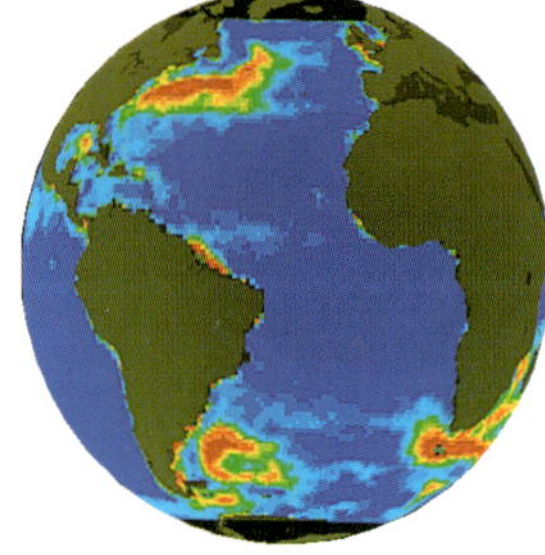

Oceanography

The study of the oceans is called oceanography. It covers ocean chemistry, the ocean bed and currents (shown above by satellite), and marine life.

Geography

This is the study of the Earth's surface. Human geography looks at world patterns of human activity; physical geography studies the Earth's physical environment.

Meteorology

The atmosphere is studied within the discipline of meteorology. This focuses on the processes that make the weather, and on weather forecasting. Climatology is the study of weather patterns.

Surveying the Earth

Earth scientists can learn very little about the Earth from laboratory studies. Instead, they must make observations, collect data, and test their theories in the outside world – this may mean climbing mountains or braving earthquakes. Satellite photography has provided a vast new source of data, but most information continues to come from field work.

Survey equipment

Earth scientists sometimes need to use specific survey equipment. This laser equipment helps to monitor the movement of earthquakes.

Earth resources

The Earth provides all the materials we need for living, from the food we eat and the water we drink, to the bricks we use for building. Earth sciences help us to identify the location of these resources. They also show what damage we may be doing to them by exploiting them thoughtlessly.

Air

We need air to breathe virtually every second of our lives. However, this vital resource is becoming increasingly damaged by human pollution.

Tourmaline gemstone

Minerals

From metal for cars to concrete for buildings, nearly everything we make comes from the minerals or chemicals taken from the Earth's crust. Gems are another of its rich resources.

Water

All forms of life are dependent on water. Patterns of human activity are controlled by the need to be near a source of clean water.

Fruit

Squid

Food

Food is provided by things living on the Earth's surface. These depend on the mineral resources, water, and air provided by the Earth.

Energy

Ninety per cent of the energy we use comes from a finite supply of minerals – oil, coal, and gas – extracted from the Earth's crust.

FIND OUT MORE

CLIMATE · EARTH · FOSSILS · GEOLOGY · OCEANS AND SEAS · ROCKS AND MINERALS · VOLCANOES · WEATHER

ECOLOGY AND ECOSYSTEMS

NO LIVING THING exists in isolation. It interacts with other living things and with its physical surroundings. The study of these relationships is called ecology. Ecologists consider all the organisms that live in one area as an inter-dependent community. All plants and animals rely on, and influence, vital factors in their environment, such as the supply of nutrients, food, and water. A community and its environment is called an ecosystem.

Communities

Wildlife communities exist almost everywhere you look, on land, in rivers, and in the oceans. A typical community contains a mixture of plants, various animals that feed on them or hunt one another, and organisms that burrow through the soil debris below.

Trees offer shelter for animals, and food in the form of leaves, berries, seeds, and blossom.

Insects feeding on flowers help to pollinate them.

Habitats

The habitat of a species is the surroundings in which it lives, including the rocks, soils, water, and plants. Different habitats are suitable for different species and have a certain type of community.

Mice eat seeds, and are hunted by bigger animals.

Dense undergrowth provides shelter for small animals.

Most of the tadpoles that hatch out from the frog spawn will be food for other animals.

Rotting wood is home to fungi and invertebrates.

Snails feed on the leaves of plants and are food for some birds such as thrushes.

As ferns grow, they take nutrients from the soil.

Frogs live in both land and water habitats.

Biomes

The biggest ecological units are biomes, such as deserts, rainforests, and lakes, across which similar climatic and other conditions create similar ecosystems. The plants and animals may differ across a biome, but they make up the same sort of communities with the same ecological features.

Seashores

Battered by waves and flooded by tides, seashores have few plants other than seaweeds. Animals include shellfish, rockpool fish, and wading birds.

Deserts

Cloud-free, dry climates create deserts. These are home only to plants and animals that are able to cope with extremes of aridity and temperature.

Grassland

Grassland is normal in places where there is a long dry season. It can support lots of grazing animals, some preyed on by swift-running predators. The savannah of East Africa is one of the best-known areas of grassland.

Rainforests

In hot, humid climates, dense forests develop that are home to a huge variety of animal life. Tropical rainforests cover only 10 per cent of the Earth's land surface, but contain more than half of all animal and plant species.

Ecosystems

An ecosystem contains several different wildlife communities and their habitat. Ecologists use the term to mean all the complicated interactions that take place among living and non-living things in an area. The various components of the ecosystem include sunshine, water, nutrients in the soil, bacteria, plants, and animals.

Freshwater

Lake- and river-dwelling communities include floating or submerged plants, freshwater plankton, and fish. Different species live in different parts of a river or lake, depending on the conditions that they tolerate. This is Bow Lake in the Canadian Rockies.

Ecological interactions

The components of an ecosystem interact with each other in lots of different ways. Rain, for example, provides water for plants. Plant growth and decay affect the form and content of soil. Soil provides a home for worms, and worms, as they move about, change the structure of the soil.

Puss moth larva cuts and chews leaves, using its sharp jaws.

Toucans live high in the crowns of trees.

Food

Perhaps the most obvious way in which living species affect one another's lives is by feeding. Most things are food for something else. For example, caterpillars eat leaves, but are themselves food for animals such as birds. The birds are food for other animals, and so on up the food chain.

Shelter

The cover and shelter that trees and vegetation provide offer much more security than bare, open ground. In a rainforest, the large trees provide toucans with shelter from the weather, a place where they can raise their young in relative safety, and protection from predators.

Pollen sac

Bumblebees collect nectar with their tongue.

Transport

Animals can move around whereas plants cannot. Plants, therefore, use various methods that ensure animals carry their seeds and pollen, so that a new generation of plants can develop and grow. Bumblebees carry pollen on their legs.

Honey fungus

Young stinkhorn fungus

Parasitism

Animals, plants, and fungi that live off other living things are called parasites. Nearly all animals and plants are host to parasites of some kind. A parasitic relationship exists between a honey fungus and a tree. The fungus steals food from the tree, usually harming it in the process.

Symbiosis

When two species have a close relationship in which both benefit, it is called symbiotic. Symbiosis often involves giving shelter in return for protection or food, and it occurs among all kinds of organisms.

Clownfish

Clownfish find shelter among the stinging tentacles of sea anemones, which do not harm them. The fish may lure in other fish for the anemones to consume.

Clownfish stay where they are protected.

Adaptation

All plants and animals are specially suited to live in their particular habitat. How they become suited, or adapted, is the key to evolution. How and where a species lives, how it gets its food, what it eats, and how it interacts with others, is known as its ecological niche.

Spines protect the swollen stem.

Cacti

A cactus has adapted in many ways to desert life. For example, its leaves have adapted into spines, to prevent water from evaporating too easily. When rain does fall, a cactus stores as much water as possible in its stem.

Cycles in nature

Nature automatically recycles the substances that are vital for life. Oxygen, nitrogen, carbon, and water are constantly being exchanged between the air, the soil, the oceans, and living things. If substances were not continuously put back into the ecosystems to be used again, the supply for organisms would soon run out and life would stop.

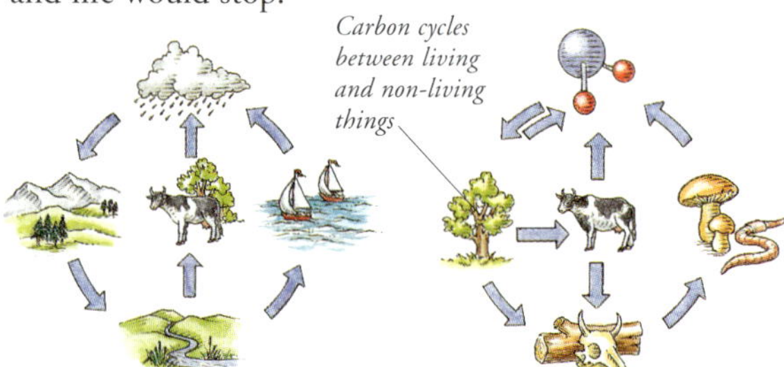

Carbon cycles between living and non-living things.

Water cycle

Water lost by evaporation from plants, rivers, and seas, forms clouds in the atmosphere. This falls back as rain, runs into rivers and seas, and is soaked up from the soil by the roots of plants.

Carbon cycle

Organisms release carbon dioxide into the air. Carbon is also released when organisms decay, or when coal is burned. Plants absorb carbon from the air, which passes into animals that eat them.

Ecological change

Ecosystems do not always stay the same but may change over time. If an event changes the landscape, for example, high winds create a clearing in a wood, first grasses and herbs grow, then shrubs colonize the plot until trees take over once again.

The process of change from grassland to woodland is called succession.

Land erosion in Madagascar

Human impact

People's actions also change ecosystems and often the impact is so great that nature cannot repair the damage. For example, poor farming techniques sometimes cause so much soil to be eroded away from the land, that plants cannot get established and the vegetation can never recover.

FIND OUT MORE: ANIMAL BEHAVIOUR · EVOLUTION · FOOD WEBS AND CHAINS · POLLUTION · SOIL

ECUADOR AND PERU

TOGETHER ECUADOR AND PERU form the western side of equatorial South America, lying between Colombia to the north, Chile to the south, and Brazil and Bolivia to the east. The dominant influences in the west of the region were the Incas, who ruled until the 1500s, and the conquering Spaniards, who imposed their own culture and language. About 40 per cent of the population are *mestizos*, who are people of mixed blood resulting from intermarriage between Spaniards and Incas. Many Native Americans still live in remote Amazonian villages.

Physical features

Lying on South America's Pacific Coast, Ecuador and Peru are dominated by the jagged volcanic peaks of the Andes, whose eastern slopes descend to the hot, humid, tropical rainforest and wetlands of the Amazon Basin. To the west is the coastal strip. Peru's coast is largely arid desert, but Ecuador's coast is hot, swampy, or forested.

Mount Cotopaxi

A perfect cone capped with snow, Cotopaxi, 5,897 m (19,345 ft) is the world's highest active volcano and Ecuador's second highest peak. It lies in the Andes, which form the backbone of both Ecuador and Peru. Ecuador has 15 major volcanoes, ten of which are active. The whole region is shaken from time to time by earthquakes, which cause damage to cities.

A B C D E F G H
1 2 3 4 5 6 7 8 9 10 11
COLOMBIA
ECUADOR
PERU
BRAZIL
BOLIVIA
CHILE
PACIFIC OCEAN
Esmeraldas
Ibarra
Equator
QUITO
Santo Domingo de los Colorados
Cotopaxi 5897 m
Latacunga
Manta
Portoviejo
Ambato
Montecristi
Riobamba
Babahoyo
Milagro
Guayaquil
Gulf of Guayaquil
Cuenca
Machala
Loja
Aguarico
Napo
Putumayo
Amazon Basin
Amazon
Iquitos
Ramón Castilla
Marañón
Sullana
Piura
Moyobamba
Chiclayo
Tarapoto
Cajamarca
Ucayali
Trujillo
Pucallpa
Chimbote
Huaraz
Huánuco
Cerro de Pasco
Tarma
La Oroya
Callao
LIMA
Huancayo
Apurímac
Madre de Dios
Machu Picchu
Ayacucho
Cusco
Andes
Ica
Nazca
San Juan
L. Titicaca
Juliaca
Puno
Arequipa
Mollendo
Moquegua
Tacna
0 km 250
0 miles 250

Lake Titicaca

At more than 170 km (106 miles) long, Lake Titicaca is South America's largest lake. The Uros people live here on islands that they make from the *totora* reed. They also make reed boats.

Amazon Basin

The steamy Amazon Basin occupies the eastern regions of Ecuador and Peru. The forest is not an uninterrupted mass of trees, but contains pockets of grassland and swamps. The headwaters of the Amazon originate in this region. Much of this area is disputed territory awarded to Peru in 1942.

Regional climate

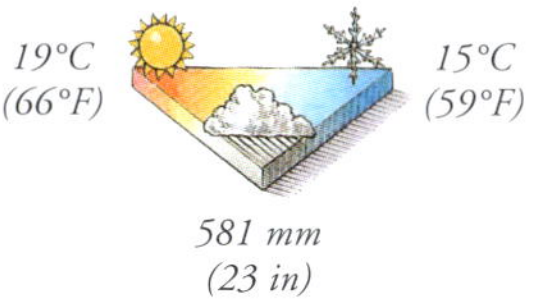

Ecuador is hot and humid along the coast, cool and fresh in the Andes, and hot with heavy rainfall in the Amazon Basin. Peru has a more mixed climate. The coastal region is dry, and kept cool by the cold waters of the Peru Current. The western part of the Peruvian Andes is fairly dry, but the eastern Andes and tropical Amazonia have heavy rainfall.

Picking coca leaves, Quillabamba, Peru

Coca

The Incas used to chew coca leaves to relieve fatigue and hunger. Today, in remote areas, coca is grown illegally to produce the powerful and dangerous drug cocaine for supply to the international drug trade. Governments are offering farmers money to destroy their coca crops and grow bananas, cocoa, or coffee instead.

Ecuador

The third smallest, most densely populated independent country in South America, Ecuador is also one of the most geographically varied and politically stable. Agriculture and oil dominate the economy. About 1,000 km (630 miles) off Ecuador's Pacific coast, the lonely Galápagos Islands, famous for their unique wildlife, are part of the country.

Quechua woman gathering gladioli for market

People

Native Americans make up 25 per cent and *mestizos* more than 50 per cent of the population. The rest of the people are white, black, or Asian. More than 93 per cent of the people are Roman Catholic, although some people blend Catholicism with traditional beliefs.

Ecuador Facts

Capital city	Quito
Area	283,560 sq km (109,483 sq miles)
Population	12,900,000
Main languages	Spanish, Quechua
Major religion	Christian
Currency	US dollar

Oil

Since the 1970s, oil, piped from the eastern lowlands, has been the mainstay of Ecuador's economy and accounts for 40 per cent of exports. Other exports are balsa wood, shrimps, processed fish, and textiles. Most goods are exported via Guayaquil, Ecuador's main port and largest city.

Crops

Beans, maize, and potatoes are the main crops grown in the Andes. Bananas, cocoa beans, rice, coffee, oranges, and wheat are cultivated on the coast, mostly for export. Roses, carnations, gladioli, and statice (sea lavender) are grown for markets.

Bold rug designs, often with an animal theme, are woven from homespun wool fibre.

Otavalo market

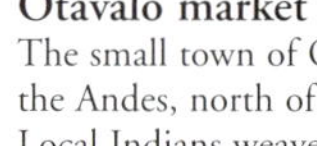

The small town of Otavalo lies high in the Andes, north of the capital Quito. Local Indians weave brightly coloured ponchos and rugs to sell at the famous Otavalo market, which dates from pre-Inca times.

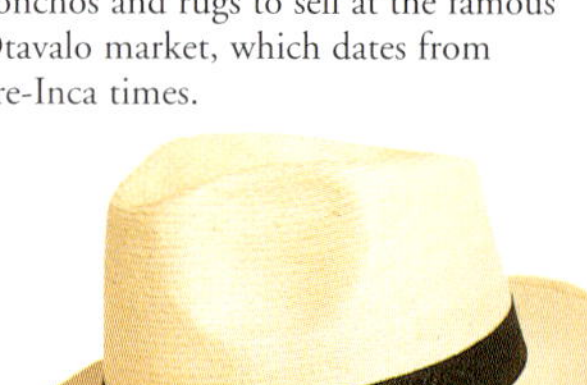

Panama hats

Originally made in the 1800s in Ecuador, to protect the heads of travellers, panama hats are constructed from the fibres of the toquilla plant. A panama can be rolled up for packing – a good one will pass through a finger ring.

Peru

Four hundred years ago, Peru was at the heart of the Inca Empire, ruins of which still survive high in the Andes. The country has great mineral resources, yet most Peruvians are poor farmers, growing potatoes, maize, rice, and cereals for their own use, and cotton and coffee for export. Political terrorism by the Maoist Shining Path group has forced military rule in some areas.

Machu Picchu

Peru's greatest tourist attraction is the ruined Inca city of Machu Picchu in the Andes. The ruins, hidden by dense forest vegetation, were discovered in 1911, when American archaeologist Hiram Bingham stumbled upon them, almost by accident. The ruins are made of stone and were built without mortar.

Peru Facts

Capital city	Lima
Area	1,285,220 sq km (496,223 sq miles)
Population	26,100,000
Main languages	Spanish, Quechua, Aymara
Major religion	Christian
Currency	Nuevo sol (new sol)

Railways

Peru has two unconnected railway networks – the Central and Southern Railroads – both of which go from the coast to the highlands. A branch of the Central Railroad linking Lima and Huancayo in the Andes reaches 4,818 m (15,806 ft) above sea-level, making it the highest standard-gauge line in the world.

People

About half of Peruvians are Native American, and one-third are *mestizo*. The most populated areas are the highlands and the coastal plain. Only five per cent of people live in the remote Amazon Basin areas, including 70 Native American groups.

Jivaro man

Fishing

The cold waters of the Peru coastal current bring rich nutrients that attract large numbers of pilchards, sardines, tuna, and other fish, making fishing a major industry in Peru. However, every few years, the arrival of the El Niño current raises the temperature of the water driving away the fish and causing great hardship to the fishermen.

Sardines

Mining

Peru is a leading producer of copper, lead, tungsten, silver, and zinc and has reserves of gold, iron ore, and oil. However, low world mineral prices and industrial problems have badly affected mining.

Opencast lead mine in the Andes

Farming | Fishing industry | Incas | Native Americans | Oil | Pacific Ocean | Rocks and minerals | South America, history of | Textiles and weaving | Trains and railways | Volcanoes

EDISON, THOMAS

ONE OF THE GREATEST INVENTORS of all time, Thomas Alva Edison produced a number of inventions that changed the world – electric lighting, sound recording, and an early form of moving pictures, among many others. He had little formal schooling, but he was fascinated by science. He worked extremely hard, and would spend days, months, or even years experimenting in order to make something work. He often slept fully clothed on one of his worktables, so that he could start work again first thing in the morning.

Early life

Edison was born in 1847 in a small town in Ohio, USA. His teachers thought he was stupid, so his mother taught him herself, inspiring his interest in science. In 1869, after moving to New York, he improved the "ticker", a machine for relaying information about the stock market. The machine earned him $40,000.

Menlo Park

In 1876, using the money from his stock "ticker", Edison built an "invention factory" at Menlo Park, 39 km (24 miles) from New York City. This barn-like two-storey building was the world's first research laboratory, where a staff of scientists helped Edison to develop his ideas into devices that actually worked. In the six years that Edison worked at Menlo Park, he patented more than 400 different inventions.

Research work

At Menlo Park, Edison would come up with rough ideas and sketches. These would be refined, built, and tested by his assistants. They often had to build inventions again and again to find out why they did not work. Edison, when asked about his success, stressed the importance of these setbacks. "I failed my way to success," he said.

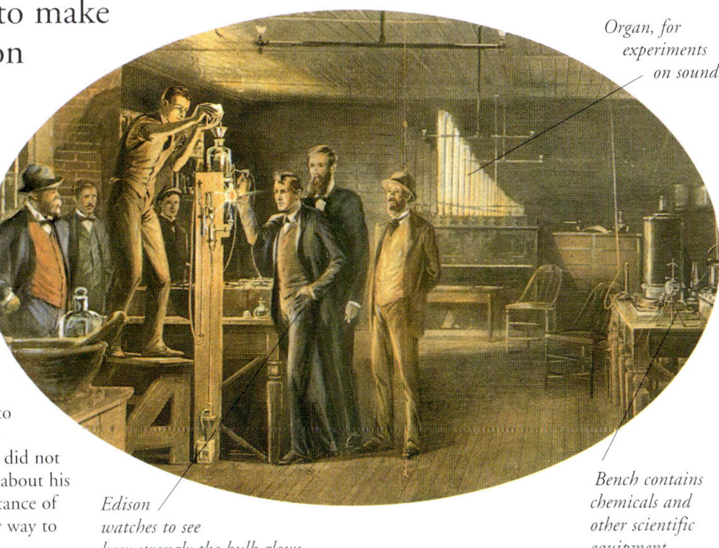

Organ, for experiments on sound

Edison watches to see how strongly the bulb glows.

Bench contains chemicals and other scientific equipment.

Electric light

Perhaps Edison's most important invention was the electric lightbulb. He saw that a bulb with a glowing thread or filament would work, using little electricity. It took him thousands of experiments before he discovered that the best material for the filament was carbonized cotton thread. British scientist Joseph Swan (1828–1914) invented a lightbulb at the same time as Edison, and the two men later joined forces.

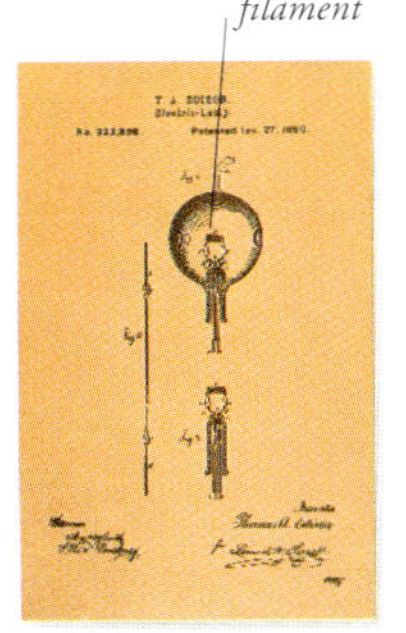

Carbon filament

Patent drawing for the lightbulb

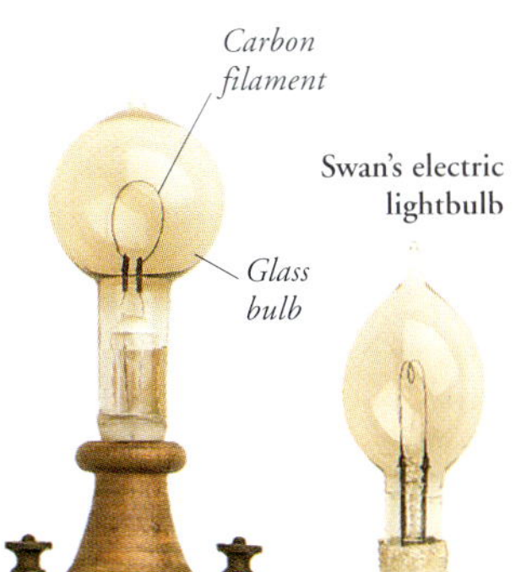

Carbon filament

Glass bulb

Edison's electric lightbulb

Swan's electric lightbulb

Lighting the city

Having developed the lightbulb, Edison went on to create a complete electric lighting system, powered by a central generator. His first power plant opened in 1882, serving 85 satisfied customers. Soon, whole cities were lit with electricity.

Other inventions

Edison patented 1,093 inventions in his lifetime. He helped make the first successful typewriter, a dictating machine, and an improved telephone mouthpiece. He came close to inventing radio, and predicted the use of atomic power.

Recording cylinder

Mouthpiece

Handle to turn cylinder

Edison's phonograph

Phonograph

The phonograph, a device for recording and playing back sounds, was Edison's favourite invention. He sketched the machine and gave it to an assistant to build. It worked, but Edison did not realize this because he had poor hearing.

Recording the voice

Kinetoscope

In 1889, Edison invented the kinetoscope, a projector with a peepshow-type viewer to go with it. Kinetoscopes were installed in special viewing parlours in the USA, and customers paid to watch short films.

THOMAS EDISON

1847 Born, Milan, Ohio, USA.

1869 Improves the "ticker", for relaying prices on the stock market.

1876 Moves to Menlo Park.

1877 Creates the phonograph.

1877 Invents the carbon microphone, for use in telephone mouthpieces.

1879 Patents the electric lightbulb.

1882 Power switched on at the Pearl Street generating station, New York.

1883 Edison and Swan form an electric company.

1889 Invents the kinetoscope.

1931 Dies, aged 84.

FIND OUT MORE
ELECTRICITY · FILMS AND FILM-MAKING · INVENTIONS · PHYSICS · SCIENCE, HISTORY OF · SOUND RECORDING · TECHNOLOGY

EDUCATION

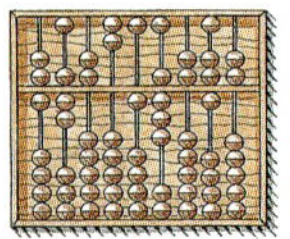

FOR A SOCIETY TO SURVIVE and progress, each generation must pass its knowledge, skills, and values on to the next. This process is called education. Passing on knowledge is so vital that most countries have established formal systems of education for teaching children, by sending them to schools and colleges. Throughout our lives we are also educated informally, by parents, friends, or the media. Education provides society with doctors, teachers, and scientists; gives industry a capable workforce; and helps maintain law and order by instructing people in social values.

Early education

In prehistoric times, elders taught children the survival skills they needed, such as how to hunt or make fire. As civilizations developed and writing was invented, formal institutions of learning – schools – were created so that some people could learn to read and write.

The ancient world

As happens today, education in the ancient world reflected the state's needs and attitudes. In warlike Sparta, for example, education was geared towards producing good soldiers. Throughout the ancient world and medieval Europe, women and the poor did not have the same acccess to education enjoyed by the male, ruling classes.

Teacher and pupil, Romano-Germanic period

Theories of education

Some theories state that people learn by practice; others, that pupils must work things out themselves in order to learn; and some suggest that pupils learn by following their emotional needs and acquiring the skills and knowledge to fulfil them. Most people probably learn in all three ways.

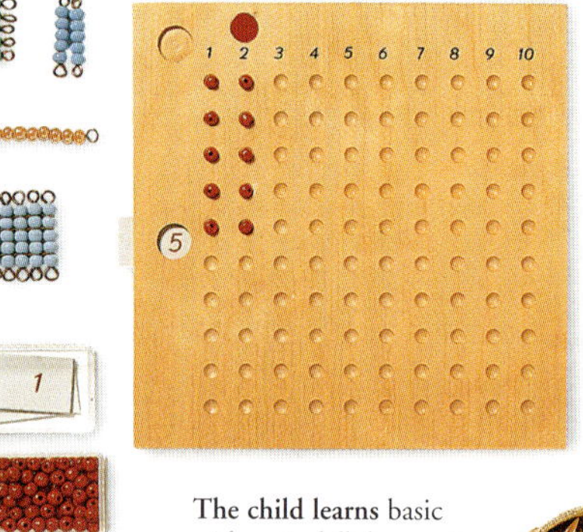

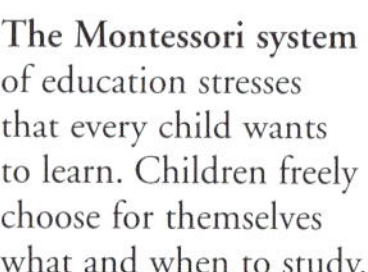

Beads in number units

The child learns basic arithmetic skills by creative play with special, three-dimensional equipment.

The Montessori system of education stresses that every child wants to learn. Children freely choose for themselves what and when to study.

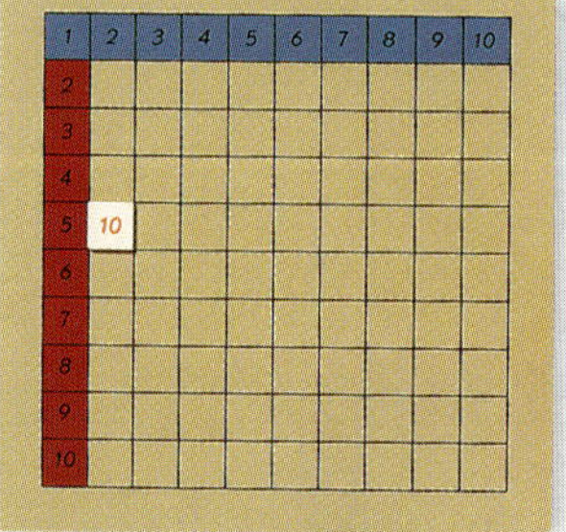

Multiplication board

Socialization

The first form of education a child receives starts from birth, by his or her immediate carers. Known as socialization, it includes not only learning such basic skills as speaking, but also teaches the child how society expects that he or she should behave. The child learns from instruction, and by imitating others. Socialization also takes place at school, and through cultural influences such as television.

Table manners are a learnt form of social behaviour.

Types of education

Different types of education cater for different needs. The best-known example is the general education that schools and colleges provide, in subjects such as reading, writing, and arithmetic.

Mother teaches sewing skills to children.

Vocational

Vocational education prepares people for specific jobs; it is available through courses at school, or training at specific colleges. Skills or crafts are also passed on informally, perhaps from parent to child, when a trade is passed on from one generation to the next.

Adult education

Adult education is for those who, although not full-time students, choose to continue an aspect of their education, or learn something new. The courses keep adults up-to-date, improve job prospects, and bring new interests.

Learning computer skills

Disabled boy learns sailing skills.

Special needs

Wealthy nations can afford to provide some schools where education is tailored to the special needs of certain children, such as the physically challenged or the highly gifted.

Maria Montessori

The Italian educationist Maria Montessori (1870–1952) developed teaching methods that encouraged children to work things out for themselves through practical activity, rather than simply obeying instructions. She developed her ideas while working with children with learning difficulties.

Timeline

c.3100 BC Sumerians invent writing.

3rd century BC Greek thinker Plato (c.427 BC–c.347 BC) proposes that education should be run by the state.

1524 German priest Martin Luther (1483–1546) advocates education be made available for all, so that everyone is able to read the Bible.

1762 French philosopher Jean Jacques Rousseau (1712–78) argues education should prepare children to be adults.

1763 Prussians introduce compulsory schooling from the ages of 5 to 13.

1899 US educator John Dewey (1859–1952) publishes *The School and Society*, an influential analysis of the social function of education.

1945 World War II ends: with the desire to build a better world, many countries reform school systems to make secondary education available to all.

1990s Education is fully recognized as vital to social and economic growth.

FIND OUT MORE
CRIME AND PUNISHMENT
SCHOOLS AND COLLEGES
SOCIETIES, HUMAN
TRADE AND INDUSTRY
WRITING

EGGS

MANY KINDS OF ANIMAL, from earthworms and insects to fish and birds, reproduce by laying eggs. An egg is a single living cell complete with a supply of food. After the egg is laid, the cell starts to divide, and gradually a young animal's body takes shape. When the animal is ready to start life in the world outside, it breaks out of the egg, or hatches. There is a great variety of eggs – large and small, with shells and without. Some animals lay just a few eggs each time and look after them carefully. Others lay thousands or millions of eggs and leave them to develop on their own.

Types of egg

Some eggs are so small that they can be seen only under a microscope; others are as big and heavy as a coconut. Animals that live in water usually lay jelly-like eggs. Animals that live on land, such as insects, reptiles, and birds, lay eggs with a hard or leathery shell. The shell helps to stop an egg drying out.

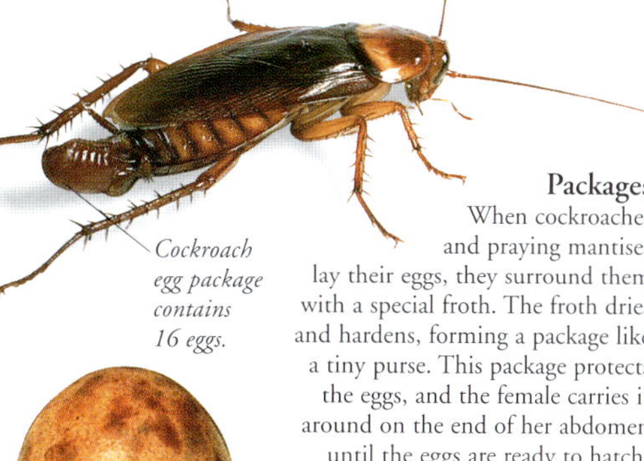

Cockroach egg package contains 16 eggs.

Packages

When cockroaches and praying mantises lay their eggs, they surround them with a special froth. The froth dries and hardens, forming a package like a tiny purse. This package protects the eggs, and the female carries it around on the end of her abdomen until the eggs are ready to hatch.

Eggs without a shell

Frogs' eggs do not have a shell. Instead, they are surrounded by a layer of jelly. The jelly swells up when the eggs are laid, forming a floating mass that can be more than 30 cm (12 in) across.

Eggs in strings

The common toad lays eggs like those of frogs, but they are laid in strings up to 3 m (10 ft) long. As the female lays the eggs, she winds them around underwater plants. The tadpoles hatch after about two weeks.

Leopard gecko's egg

Leathery eggs

Lizards and many other reptiles have eggs with a leathery shell. Unlike amphibians, reptiles can lay their eggs in dry places, because the shell helps keep the inside of the egg moist.

American robin's egg

Leatherhead's egg

Chalky eggs

The shell around birds' eggs is reinforced with a substance like chalk. To hatch, most young birds peck open their shell, but some kick their way out.

Mermaids' purses

Sharks lay some of the most unusual eggs. Instead of being round, their eggs can be flat, or even spiral. Dogfish, which are small sharks, lay eggs called "mermaids' purses". These have long tendrils with which the dogfish anchors the eggs to underwater plants.

Egg development

After an egg has been laid, a young animal starts to develop inside it. With some insects, such as the housefly, this can take less than a day, but with birds it may take more than a month. Eggs develop more quickly if they are warm, and most birds keep their eggs warm by sitting on them. This is called incubation.

Mallee fowl

Instead of sitting on its eggs, the Australian mallee fowl buries them in a huge compost heap that it makes out of dead leaves. Heat from the giant heap keeps the eggs warm.

Development of a bird's egg

A bird's egg is divided into two main areas – the white and the yolk. The white is made of a substance called albumen. It stores water and cushions the developing chick from any sudden jolts. The yolk contains a store of food, which the chick uses up as it develops.

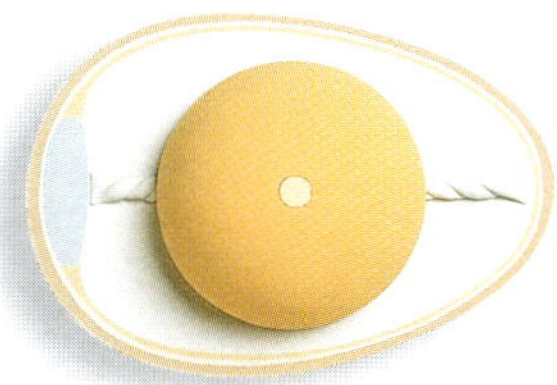

1 When the egg has just been laid, the part that will become the chick looks like a tiny pale spot. It lies on the upper surface of the yolk.

2 Within a day, cells in the spot start to divide to form an embryo. A network of blood vessels fans out over the yolk and supplies the embryo with food.

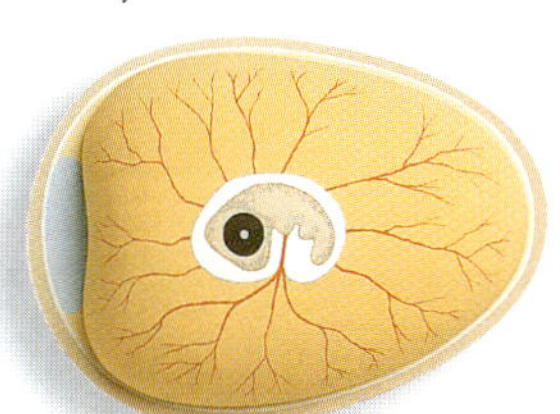

3 Three days after the egg was laid, the embryo is growing fast. Its eyes start to form, and tiny buds grow that will soon develop into wings and legs.

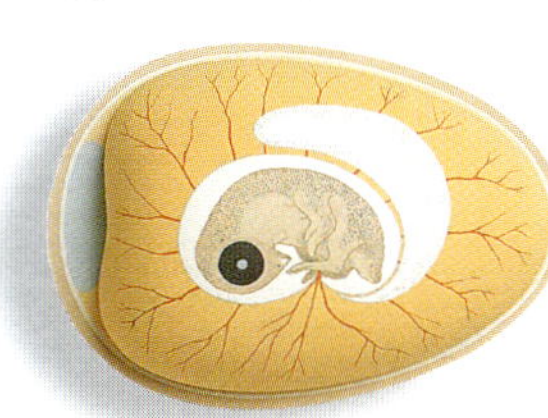

4 After seven days, the embryo has become a chick, and a special bag has formed to collect its waste. In three weeks, the chick's development will be complete.

Egg clutches

Some animals, such as queen termites, lay a steady stream of eggs, but most animals produce eggs in groups called clutches. The number of eggs in a clutch is closely linked to their size. For example, a wandering albatross has very big eggs, but it produces only one egg every two years. By contrast, a sunfish has tiny eggs, but it releases millions each time it breeds.

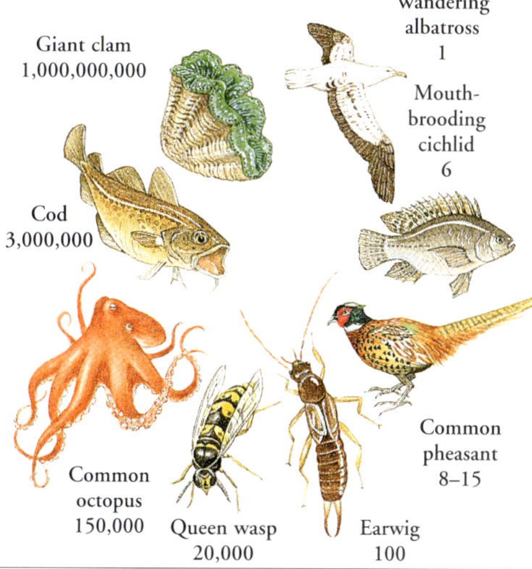

Eggs

Non-passerine birds

Glossy ibis eggs are not camouflaged.

Willow grouse eggs are laid on the ground where they are camouflaged.

Plains wanderer lays eggs in a grass-lined hollow.

Jamaican tody eggs are almost spherical and have an extremely thin shell.

Black shouldered kite eggs often have marks concentrated at one end.

Guira cuckoo eggs are, unusually for cuckoos, incubated by the parents.

Common guillemot eggs are sharply pointed.

Limpkin eggs are camouflaged to blend in with dead leaves of waterside plants.

Nacunda nightjar eggs have brown blotches.

Prairie chicken lays up to 16 eggs in each clutch.

Southern cassowary eggs have a grainy surface created by raised bumps.

Manila nightjar lays its eggs on bare ground.

Elegant tinamou eggs have a glossy sheen.

Passerine birds

Olive sunbird eggs have a distinctive ring of marks.

Yellow-streaked greenbul eggs have sparse markings formed just before the egg is laid.

Cetti's warbler eggs are reddish-brown.

Bokmakierie eggs are blue with red spots.

Cape crow eggs have a large amount of red spots or speckles on them.

Paradise riflebird eggs have dark streaks that look like brush marks.

Scarlet minivet eggs have variable patterns.

Black-headed weaver eggs are laid inside a woven nest.

Black-capped mockingthrush's eggs are mottled with red spots.

Black and yellow grosbeak's eggs have streaks that may help to break up the outline.

EGYPT, ANCIENT

ABOUT 5,000 YEARS ago, the great civilization of ancient Egypt grew up on the banks of the River Nile. It lasted virtually unchanged for 3,000 years. During this time the Egyptians built the first large stone buildings, invented one of the earliest forms of writing, and created a cult of the dead unlike anything known in any other culture. This cult involved preserving dead bodies and burying them with their possessions. As a result, people today know a great deal about the ancient Egyptians.

River Nile

The River Nile was the lifeblood of the whole region. Every year the river flooded, depositing dark silt on the banks. This silt made the soil fertile and, because of this, most Egyptians lived by the river. When the Nile flooded and work in the fields was impossible, many people helped on the great royal building projects, such as the Great Pyramid at Giza.

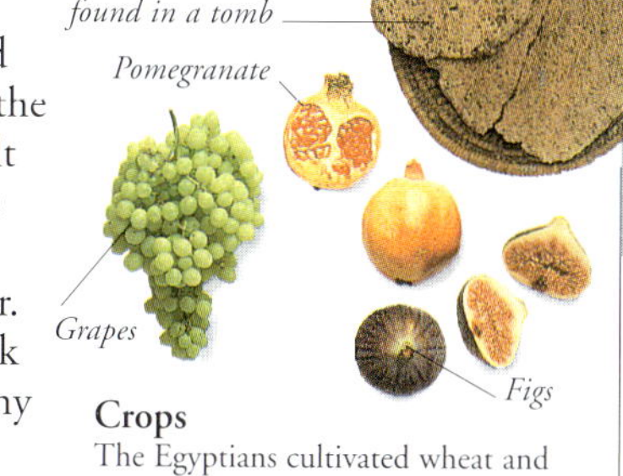

Crops
The Egyptians cultivated wheat and barley, from which they made bread and brewed beer. The hot climate also allowed them to grow many different kinds of fruit, including figs, dates, pomegranates, and grapes.

Mediterranean Sea
Nile delta
Giza
Memphis
Saqqara
Thebes
River Nile
Extent of floodplain

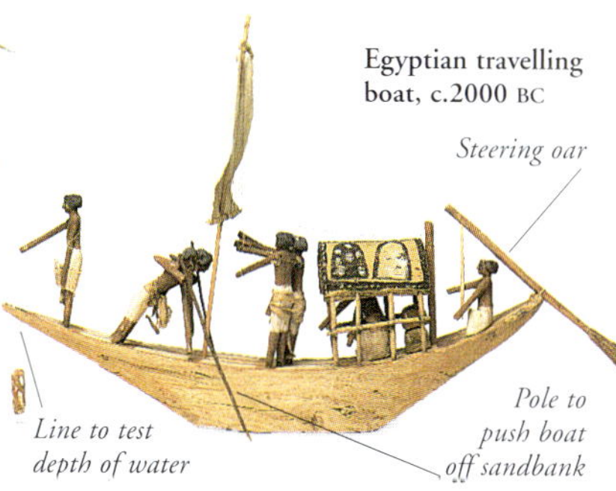

Egyptian travelling boat, c.2000 BC

Sailboats
The Nile was the main highway of Egypt. Wooden boats carried passengers and heavy cargo up and down the river. Water transport was especially useful for heavy loads, such as stones for the pyramids. Egyptian boatbuilders were among the first to attach sails to their craft.

Tilling the soil
Egyptian farmers used a lightweight plough pulled by oxen. The plough had a wooden blade and a handle so that the farmer could steer it, and was effective enough to cut a furrow in the light Egyptian soil.

Models of everyday activities, such as tilling the soil, were often found in tombs.

Egyptian farmer, c.2000 BC

Pharaohs

Ancient Egypt was ruled by kings called pharaohs. The pharaohs had absolute power, and the Egyptians believed that they joined the gods in the next world when they died. For this reason, the Egyptians took special care when burying their pharaohs, building splendid tombs.

Pharaoh's court
A pharaoh was surrounded by officials, high priests, and ambassadors, all of whom helped him run the kingdom. The court was also the home of entertainers and the women of the royal harem. The pharaoh and courtiers lived in great luxury. They took pride in their appearance, dressing in fine linen. Women used black eye make-up and had elaborate hairstyles.

Rameses II

Rameses II (r.1304–1237 BC) was famous for his military campaigns and great building projects. He defended Egypt against the Hittites, signing a peace treaty with them. His many buildings included the mortuary complex at Thebes on the west bank of the Nile, and the temple at Abu Simbel.

Gods

The Egyptians believed in many different gods. Some were local gods, who represented each district of Egypt. Others had more general powers, such as Thoth, the god of wisdom.

Anubis, the god of death

Amun-re, king of the gods

Osiris, the god of the underworld

Bast, the cat goddess

Temples
Karnak at Thebes was the greatest of the Egyptian temples. Temples were run by priests who maintained the building and left offerings for the gods. The most important temples had large estates and rich treasuries, so high priests were very powerful.

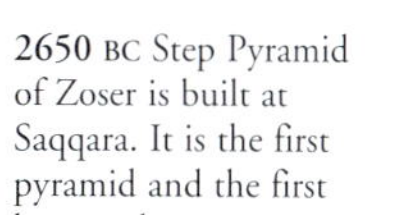

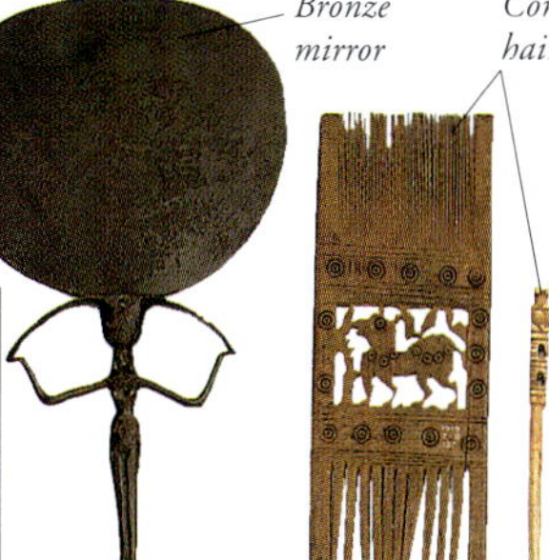

Bronze mirror

Comb and hair pins

Wine jar made from faience (decorated and glazed earthenware)

Containers for eye paint

Timeline

3000 BC Ancient Egyptian civilization begins; early Dynastic Period. The two kingdoms of Upper and Lower Egypt are united under Narmer.

2650 BC Step Pyramid of Zoser is built at Saqqara. It is the first pyramid and the first large-scale stone structure.

2500s BC Largest of the pyramids is built for Khufu at Giza.

2100 BC Middle Kingdom begins. Funerary (funeral) customs spread from royalty to other classes.

Mummification

Ancient Egyptians believed in life after death. They thought that people had a spirit as well as a body, and that for the person to live in the next world, the spirit had to be reunited with the body. They therefore preserved the body of the dead person in the form of a mummy.

Mummy cases

The Egyptians placed the mummy inside a coffin or case, and put a cover on top. By the time of the Middle Kingdom (c.2100–1550 BC), they used two coffins to give added protection from tomb robbers and animals. The coffins were decorated with writing, images of the gods, and sacred amulets, or lucky charms.

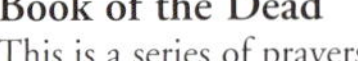

Book of the Dead

This is a series of prayers, written on papyrus, that were meant to help the dead person travel to the next world.

The Weighing of the Heart ceremony where the dead person is judged by the gods.

Thoth, the god of wisdom, writes details of the person's actions when alive.

Red straps usually indicate a priest

Linen wrappings

Making a mummy

The Egyptians first removed the organs, and dried out the body with natron. They filled the body with sawdust or dry leaves, then wrapped the body in bandages.

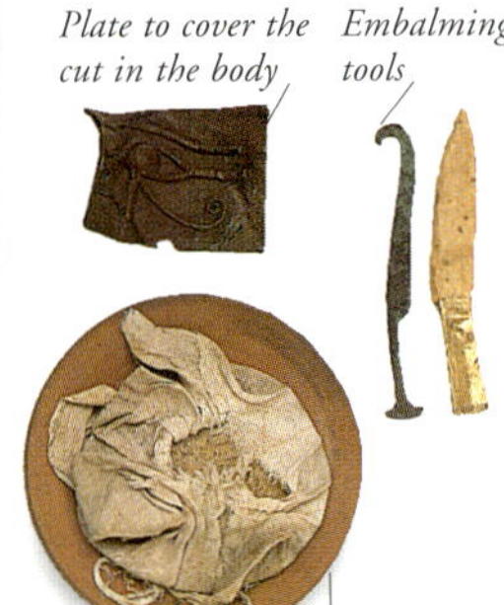

Plate to cover the cut in the body

Embalming tools

Dish of natron, a natural salt used to dry out the body.

The body's organs were placed in containers called Canopic jars.

Unwrapped mummy, showing how well preserved the body is.

Writing

Ancient Egyptians developed a complex system of writing, called hieroglyphics, in which simple pictures represented objects. Some pictures also stood for letters. Ideas that were too complicated to be shown by one picture were written as groups of hieroglyphs.

Royal door plate inscribed with the name of Amenhotep.

Hieroglyphs and hieratic script

Hieroglyphs were slow to write, so the Egyptians used them mainly for sacred texts and tomb carvings. They used another, faster script, called hieratic, for business and literary texts. Later, they invented a third script, called demotic.

Hieratic script

Hieroglyphs

Rosetta Stone

For hundreds of years, no one could read hieroglyphs. Then, in 1799, a stone slab called the Rosetta Stone was discovered. It contained the same text in hieroglyphs, demotic, and Greek. Scholars could read and understand Greek, so they could work out the meaning of the hieroglyphs.

Daily life

For most Egyptians, life consisted of hard work in the fields, and on the great building projects. They ate mainly vegetables and bread, and drank beer. High officials and royal courtiers lived a much more leisurely life.

Houses

Ancient Egyptians built houses of sun-dried mud-bricks. They covered the walls with smooth plaster. Small, high windows let in the breeze, but kept out the sun. The house pictured above belonged to a royal official, and had a garden with fruit trees.

Axe head

Axe

Chisel

Carpenter's saw

Work

Most ancient Egyptians worked at producing their own food. Others were craft workers, making items for the home from wood, pottery, and metal. Their tools, such as saws and chisels, were very similar to the hand tools used by craftworkers today.

1550 BC New Kingdom founded. Height of Egyptian civilization.

1503–1482 BC Reign of Queen Hatshepsut. She sends expeditions to the mysterious land of Punt to buy incense.

Nefertiti

1379–63 BC Reign of Akhenaten. This pharaoh, with his queen, Nefertiti, encourages realistic art, and changes Egyptian religion by banning all gods except the sun god.

1363–52 BC Brief reign of Tutankhamun, who restored the old gods but is most famous for the riches discovered in his tomb.

Tutankhamun

Abu Simbel

1304–1237 BC Reign of Rameses II, who builds Abu Simbel.

30 BC Death of Cleopatra VII; the Romans take over.

FIND OUT MORE
AFRICA, EAST | BUILDING AND CONSTRUCTION | FARMING, HISTORY OF | GODS AND GODDESSES | HITTITES | PYRAMIDS | WRITING

Ancient Egyptian amulets

Funerary amulets

Set-square amulets

Steps amulet, symbolizing the stairs on Osiris's throne.

Cartouches, containing names of the dead.

Obsidian head-rest amulets, used by ancient Egyptians instead of pillows.

Rising sun amulet, made from cornelian.

Shen amulet, symbolizing eternity

Finger amulets were placed on cuts made in the body during embalming.

Winged-heart scarab, made from faïence.

Scarabs, sacred dung beetles that represented rebirth after death.

The Ankh, the ancient Egyptian symbol of life

Wedjat eyes, representing the eye of the god Horus, were placed on mummies to protect their health.

Girdles amulets, for protecting mummies

Papyrus columns

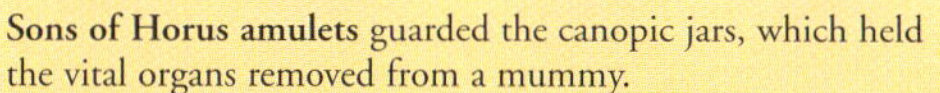

Sons of Horus amulets guarded the canopic jars, which held the vital organs removed from a mummy.

Soul-bird amulet

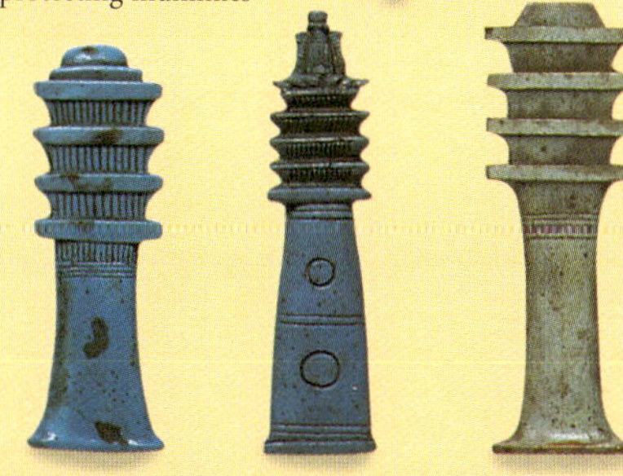

Djed pillars, amulets representing the backbone of Osiris, were thought to give the mummy strength after death.

Ushabti figures

Rensenb **Aah-mes** **Pharaoh Seti I** **Heteti** **Unnamed ushabti** **Pharaoh Merenptah**

Mummy with amulets

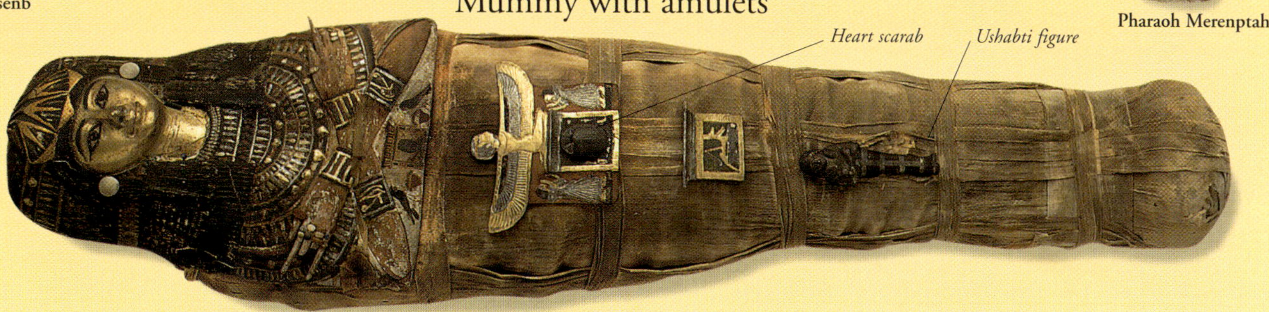

EINSTEIN, ALBERT

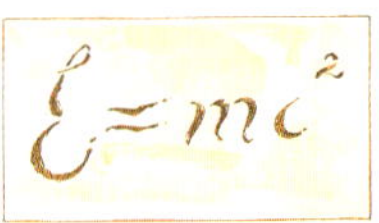

ALBERT EINSTEIN WAS a scientific genius who changed the way we view our universe. In 1905, he united space and time in one mathematical description. Ten years later he proposed a complete theory of gravity that explained how the universe works, relating mass and energy in the famous equation $E = mc^2$. Many people doubted his theories, but later investigation has since proved Einstein's theories to have been correct. As well as transforming the science of physics, Einstein's work paved the way for the creation of nuclear weapons.

Early life

Einstein was born in Ulm, Germany, and studied in Switzerland before graduating from Zurich's Institute of Technology in 1900. He did not fit in at school because he asked many difficult questions, and could get no work until he found a job in the Patent Office in Bern in 1902.

Special Theory of Relativity

In the early 1900s, Einstein developed the Special Theory of Relativity. This says that time is relative: it passes differently for individuals, depending on how fast or slowly they move. The faster anything travels, the slower time seems to pass. If one person travels into space close to the speed of light and another stays on Earth, time passes slower for the person in space. On their return, the person on Earth will be older.

Light beam sent by device on floor.

Light bounces off mirror on ceiling.

Train acts as "light clock" – the time taken by light, moving at constant speed, to go along train, acts as one "tick" of the clock.

Train appears stationary to man inside.

Light beam detected.

Man observes short "tick".

Light emitted from device on floor.

Woman sees long "tick".

Train has moved forward by time light beam hits mirror.

Train has moved still further by time light beam hits detector on floor.

Moving clocks

According to the special theory, time measured by a moving clock will run slower than if measured by a stationary clock. This can be demonstrated by light beams carried on a train travelling at nearly the speed of light. A person on the train sees the light travel a short distance; an observer on the platform sees it travel further because of the train's movement.

This light represents a pulsar.

This light represents a neutron star.

The twin stars make a double dent in spacetime.

These lines represent peaks and troughs in gravitional waves.

General Theory of Relativity

Einstein developed the General Theory of Relativity that explained gravity and the nature of space. He explained that as light travels the shortest path through space, when it bends space must be curved. Planets that travel round the Sun are thus following as straight a path as possible through curved space.

Making waves

Stars in a binary pulsar rotate round each other. As they move, they make waves in space. The waves carry energy from the stars, causing the stars to slow down as they lose energy. The rate that a pulsar slows in its orbit exactly matches Einstein's theory, though the first pulsar was not discovered until 1968.

Ripples in space

Einstein's theory predicted that objects jiggling around in space – such as two stars in a binary pulsar system – would make ripples in space. These ripples can be detected as gravitational waves. Subsequent experiments have proved Einstein's theory correct.

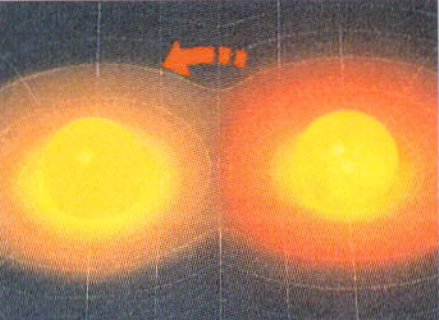

Stars rotate anti-clockwise.

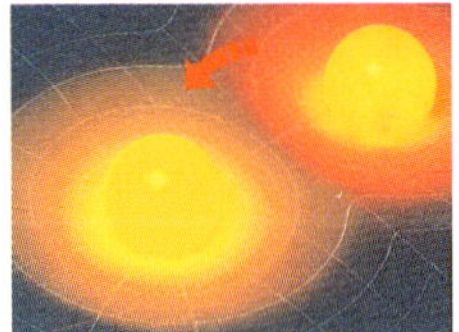

Neutron star moves around pulsar.

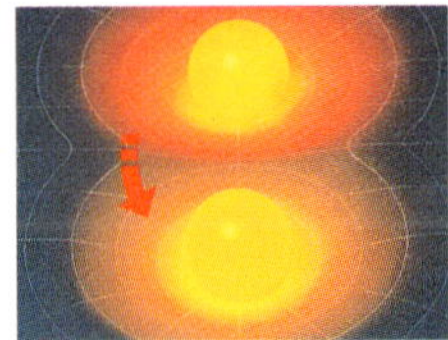

Stars' positions change in relation to observer.

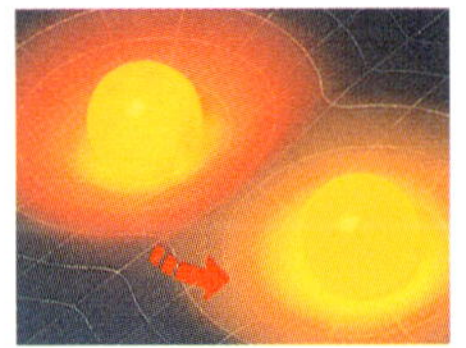

Stars continuously swap places.

Mileva Einstein

Einstein married his first wife Mileva, a mathematician and scientist, in 1903. They had a daughter and two sons. Mileva worked closely with her husband and helped with his research, though to what degree she influenced his work is unknown. They were divorced in 1919.

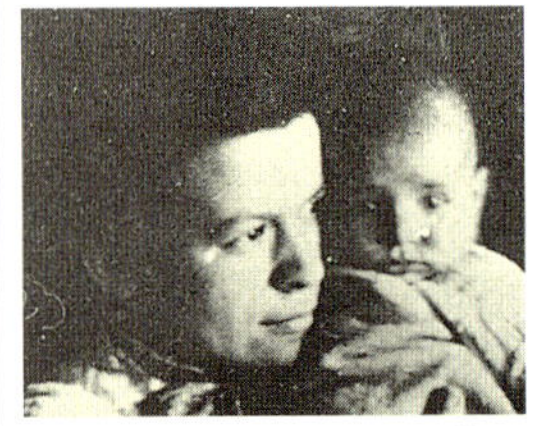

Mileva and her son Hans Albert

Political life

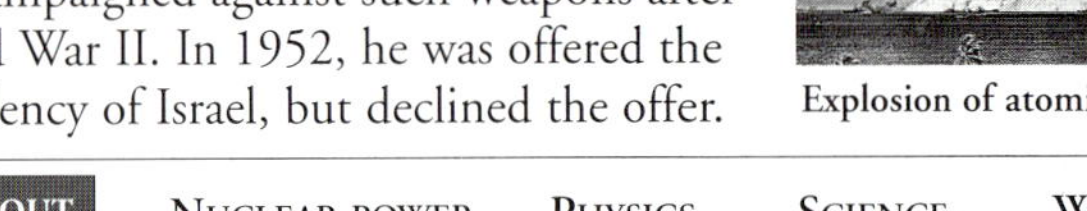

In 1933, Einstein moved to America to avoid Nazi persecution as a Jew, and campaigned for a Jewish state. He realized that his theories made possible the creation of nuclear weapons, but campaigned against such weapons after World War II. In 1952, he was offered the presidency of Israel, but declined the offer.

The bomb

In the late 1930s, Einstein feared that Nazi Germany would use nuclear weapons in war, so he wrote to US president Franklin D. Roosevelt in 1939, urging the USA to begin constructing atomic weapons to counter this threat.

Explosion of atomic bomb

ALBERT EINSTEIN

- **1879** Born in Ulm, Germany.
- **1896–1900** Studies at Institute of Technology, Zurich, Switzerland.
- **1902–9** Works in Patent Office, Bern, Switzerland.
- **1905** Obtains doctorate; writes Special Theory of Relativity.
- **1914** Moves to Berlin.
- **1915** Writes General Theory of Relativity.
- **1921** Awarded Nobel Prize for Physics.
- **1933** Moves to the USA.
- **1952** Offered presidency of Israel.
- **1955** Dies in Princeton, USA.

FIND OUT MORE
NUCLEAR POWER
PHYSICS
SCIENCE, HISTORY OF
WORLD WAR II

E

ELECTRICITY

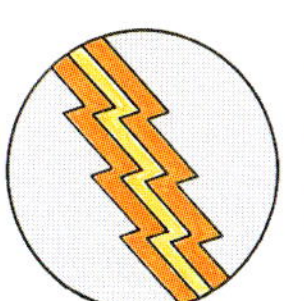

A FLASH OF LIGHTNING is striking evidence of the invisible energy called electricity. This energy is produced by the movement of electrons – tiny particles found in atoms of matter. Every electron carries an identical negative electric "charge". When electric charge builds up in one place, it is called static electricity. If the charge flows from place to place, it is called current electricity.

Electric circuit

The path around which current electricity flows is called a circuit. In the circuit shown here, electricity from the battery lights the bulbs. Two bulbs connected one after the other are described as being "in series". Bulbs in separate branches of the circuit are said to be "in parallel".

Ammeter measures current from battery.

Battery

Bulbs in series have to share the voltage, so they glow dimly.

Series circuit

Parallel circuit

Bulb in parallel gets the full voltage and glows brightly.

Voltmeter measures voltage across the bulb.

Electric current

Electrons pushed through the wires of a circuit form an electric current. The push on the electrons is called electromotive force (e.m.f). Voltage is a measure of e.m.f. The greater the voltage, the more current flows through the circuit.

Metal wire

Insulation

Electrons flow from negative charge to positive.

Battery

A battery is a source of electric current. A chemical reaction between materials in the battery separates electrons from their atoms. The battery's e.m.f makes electrons flow out of the negative terminal, around a circuit, and back to the positive terminal.

Positive terminal (+)

Ammonium chloride paste

Carbon rod

Zinc casing

Negative terminal (–)

Static electricity

Rubbing two materials together can transfer electrons from one material to the other. A material that loses electrons gains a positive charge of static electricity, and a material that gains electrons gets a negative charge.

Attracting and repelling

A positively charged balloon attracts electrons to the surface of nearby hairs, giving them a negative charge. Opposite charges attract, so the hairs are pulled towards the balloon. Charges of the same type repel (push each other away).

Lightning

A tremendous charge of static electricity builds up inside a storm cloud. A flash of lightning occurs when this charge is suddenly released as a powerful electric current.

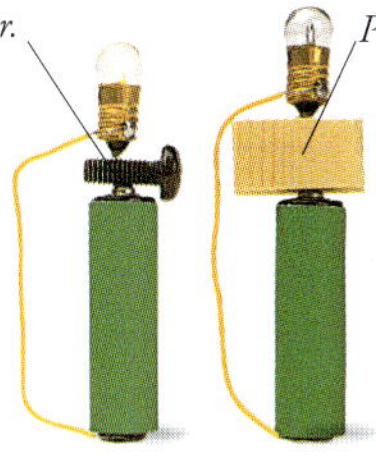

Conductors

Current can flow only through materials called conductors, whose electrons are bound loosely to their atoms and can be moved easily through the material.

Insulators

Current cannot flow through insulators. The electrons in an insulator are bound firmly to their atoms and cannot move through the material.

Generator

Most of the electricity used in homes and factories is produced by devices called generators. Inside a generator, coils of wire spin rapidly in a magnetic field. The magnetism moves electrons through the wire, creating an electric current. In this simple version, bar magnets produce the magnetic field.

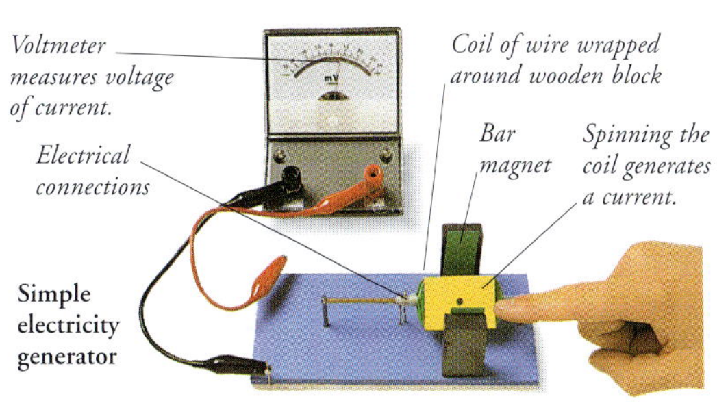

Electricity supply

Electric current produced by generators in power stations reaches consumers via cables buried underground or carried by tall towers called pylons. The current alternates, which means that it changes direction many times each second. A battery produces direct current, which flows in one direction only.

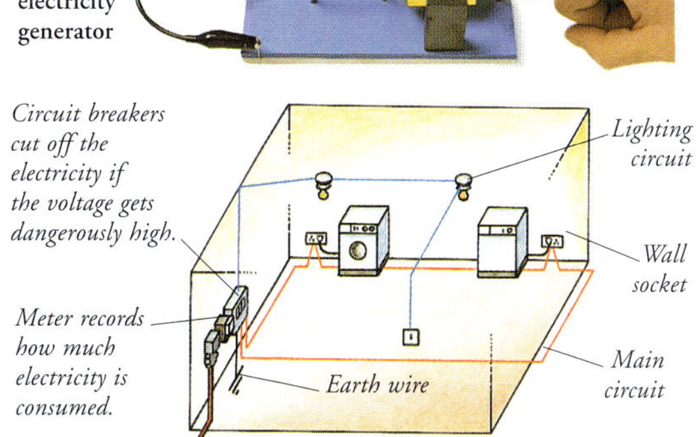

Electricity in the home

Separate circuits in the home supply different voltages for different purposes. An electrical appliance takes power from the circuits through a plug that fits into a wall socket. The sockets are linked to the ground outside by an earth wire. If an electrical fault occurs, the current is diverted safely into the ground.

Michael Faraday

In 1831, the English scientist Michael Faraday (1791–1867) built the first generator after noticing that moving a magnet in and out of a wire coil made a current flow through the wire. Faraday also invented the electric motor and pioneered electrolysis (using electricity to break down substances).

Timeline

500s BC The ancient Greeks discover static electricity when they notice that amber (fossilized tree sap) attracts small objects if rubbed with wool.

Charged amber attracting feather

1752 American scientist and politician Benjamin Franklin proves that lightning is an electrical phenomenon.

1799 Italian physicist Alessandro Volta makes the first battery.

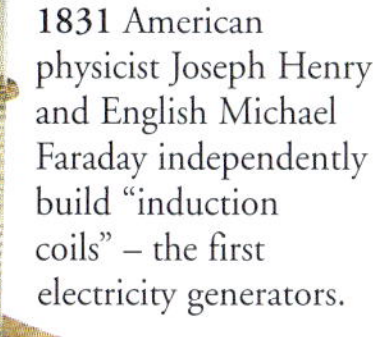

Volta's battery

1831 American physicist Joseph Henry and English Michael Faraday independently build "induction coils" – the first electricity generators.

1868 French chemist Georges Leclanché invents the Leclanché cell, the forerunner of modern zinc-carbon batteries.

1897 English physicist Joseph John Thomson discovers the electron.

FIND OUT MORE
ACIDS AND ALKALIS ELECTROMAGNETISM ENERGY FRICTION MAGNETISM STORMS

ELECTROMAGNETISM

AT THE FLICK OF A SWITCH, an invisible force turns the drum of a washing machine 1,600 times every second. This force is called electromagnetism. It is a form of magnetism produced by electricity. When an electric current flows through a wire, it produces a magnetic field around the wire. Making the wire into a coil increases the strength of the magnetic effect. Winding the coil around an iron bar makes the magnetism even stronger. Any device that exerts electromagnetic forces is called an electromagnet.

Solenoid

A coil of current-carrying wire forms a type of electromagnet called a solenoid. The magnetic field around the coil is the same as that around an ordinary bar magnet. The field's strength depends on the number of turns in the coil and the amount of current flowing through the wire.

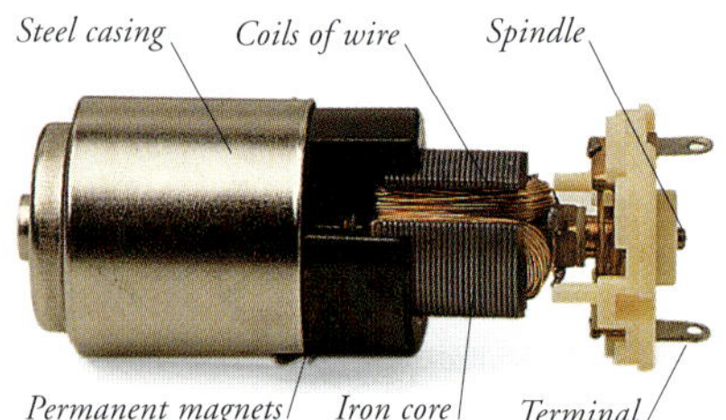

Electric motor

Inside an electric motor are wire coils surrounded by permanent magnets. Electricity flowing through the wire produces a magnetic field around each coil. The magnetism of the coils interacts with the magnetic fields of the permanent magnets. They push and pull on each other, making the coils rotate. This movement is used to drive machines such as electric drills.

Electric drill

An electric drill can quickly make a hole in wood, stone, and even some metals. Inside the body of the machine, gears harness the rotation of a powerful electric motor to drive the drill at high speed. A cooling fan prevents the drill from overheating.

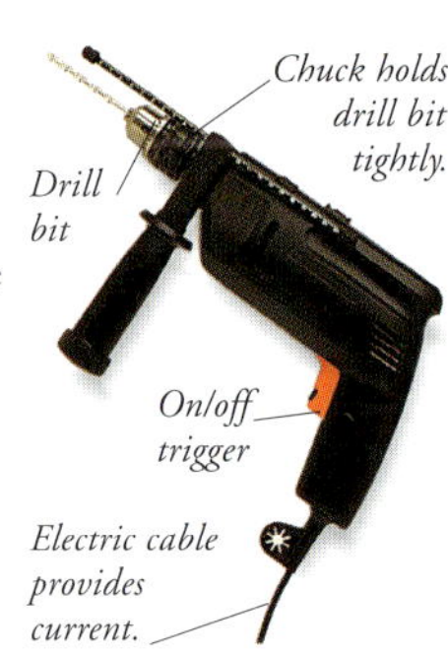

Electromagnet

Most electromagnets consist of a coil of wire wrapped around an iron bar. When an electric current flows through the wire, a magnetic field forms around the electromagnet. The magnetism can be switched off by disconnecting the electricity supply.

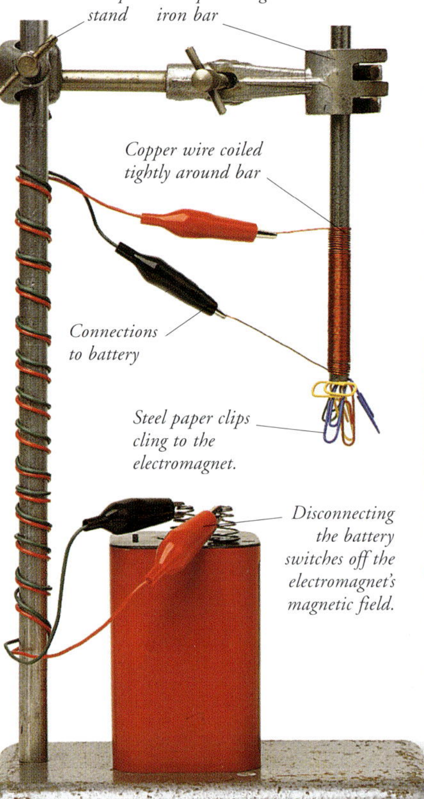

Scrapyard electromagnet

Waste metal is moved around a scrapyard by a crane carrying a huge electromagnet. When the electromagnet is switched on, it picks up metal scraps containing iron. The metal is moved to a different place and then dropped by switching off the electromagnet.

Uses of electromagnetism

Some electrical appliances contain electric motors that use electromagnetism to produce movement. But electromagnetism is also used in many other ways, such as to make sound or detect hidden objects.

Loudspeaker

A loudspeaker contains a paper or plastic cone that vibrates and creates sound waves in the air around it. The cone is attached to a wire coil surrounded by a permanent magnet. The magnetic fields of the coil and the magnet interact. This causes the coil to move rapidly to and fro, making the cone vibrate.

Metal detector

Inside the walk-through arch of an airport metal detector are large coils of wire carrying an electric current. Any person who walks under the arch passes through the magnetic field produced by the coils. A hidden metal object will affect the strength of the field and trigger an alarm.

Transformer

Many electrical devices use a transformer to alter the voltage of an electrical supply. Inside a transformer are two wire coils. When a varying current flows through one coil, it produces a varying magnetic field. This field causes an electric current to flow through the second coil, but at a different voltage.

Hans Christian Oersted

The Danish physicist Hans Christian Oersted (1777–1851) discovered electromagnetism in 1820. He placed a compass near a wire carrying an electric current and noticed that the compass needle was deflected and no longer pointed north. Oersted realized that the current had produced a magnetic field around the wire.

Timeline

1799 Italian physicist Alessandro Volta invents the battery, which allows scientists to experiment with electric currents.

1820 Oersted's discovery of electromagnetism opens the way for the development of the electric motor and the electromagnet.

Faraday's electric motor

1821 English scientist Michael Faraday makes an electric motor, in which a current-carrying wire rotates around the pole of a magnet. It has no practical use.

Sturgeon's electromagnet

1828 English scientist William Sturgeon builds the first electromagnet – a coil of wire around an insulated iron bar.

1883 Croatian-born physicist Nikola Tesla invents the "induction motor" – the first practical motor.

1885 American engineer William Stanley invents the transformer.

FIND OUT MORE
ELECTRICITY
ENGINES AND MOTORS
FORCE AND MOTION
MACHINES, SIMPLE
MAGNETISM
SOUND

ELECTRONICS

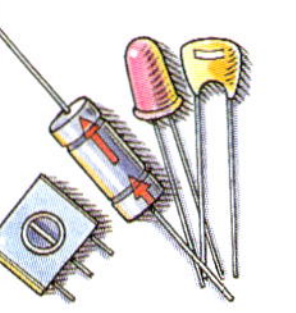

THE ELECTRONICS REVOLUTION is rapidly changing our world: whether we are at home, at work, or out shopping, we are surrounded by electronic machines and equipment. Electronics involves using devices called components to control electric currents, which are flows of tiny, electrically charged particles of matter called electrons. An electronic circuit is an arrangement of linked components – such as transistors and diodes – that manipulates current in order to carry out a specific task, such as adding numbers in a calculator.

Circuit board

The components for an electronic device, such as a radio, are attached to a circuit board, which is a flat base with metal tracks running along its underside. The components are secured to the tracks using an alloy called solder. The tracks link the components to form a circuit.

Radio circuit board and components

Inductors are wire coils that produce magnetic fields when current passes through them, creating a resistance that restricts the flow of current.

Variable capacitors can be adjusted to store varying levels of charge; in radios, they are used to select radio stations.

Diodes allow electric current to pass through them in one direction only.

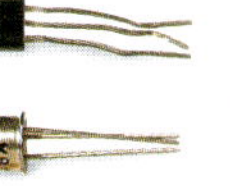

Light Emitting Diodes (LEDs) glow when current passes through them, and are used to indicate that a device's power supply is on.

Transistors can be used to amplify electrical signals (make them stronger) or switch circuits rapidly on and off.

Resistors allow only a fixed amount of electric current to flow through a circuit.

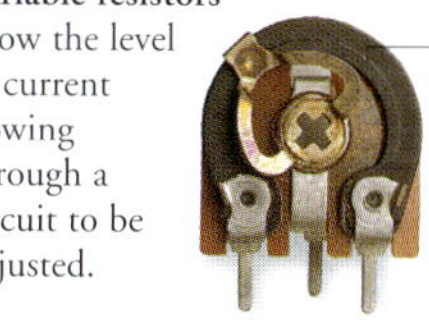

Variable resistors allow the level of current flowing through a circuit to be adjusted.

Electrolytic capacitors

Capacitors are components that store electric charge; electrolytic capacitors can store more charge than ceramic ones.

Ceramic capacitors

Power cables

Integrated circuits consist of a plastic case containing a complete circuit etched on to a tiny silicon chip.

William Shockley

US physicist William Shockley (1910–89) was part of a three-man team that invented the transistor in 1947. The transistor made it possible to build tiny electronic circuits and so develop more compact electronic devices.

Semiconductors

Silicon crystal

The element silicon is a type of material called a semiconductor, because it conducts electricity only under certain conditions. The properties of a semiconductor can be altered by adding chemical impurities to it in a process called doping. Doped semiconductors are used to make diodes, transistors, and many other electronic components.

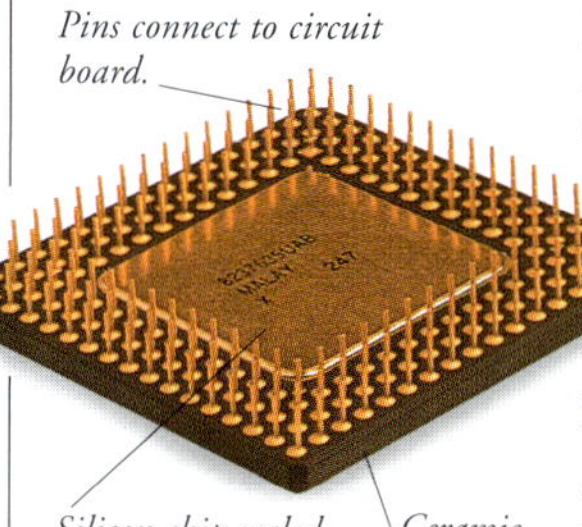

Pins connect to circuit board.

Silicon chip sealed under metal cover

Ceramic casing

Microprocessors

Many electronic devices – including computers – are controlled by circuits called microprocessors, or "silicon chips". A microprocessor is made from a single slice of doped semiconductor. The circuit, which may contain thousands of components, can carry out many complex tasks.

Uses of electronics

Electronic circuits are either analogue or digital. Analogue circuits deal with continuously varying electric currents, such as television and radio signals. Digital circuits process information in the form of thousands of on-off pulses of electric current every second.

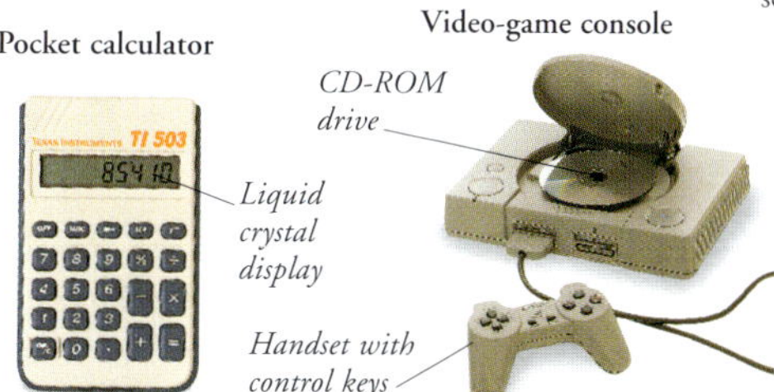

Pocket calculator

Liquid crystal display

Video-game console

CD-ROM drive

Handset with control keys

Calculator

A calculator's digital circuits split up a calculation into a series of simple steps, each of which is performed at high speed.

Video game console

Digital circuits inside the console control the play. The console sends an analogue signal to a TV screen, which displays a picture of the game.

Remote control

Pressing a button on the remote-control of a TV – for example, to change channels – makes an LED flash pulses of infrared light to the TV set. The TV set decodes the pulses and obeys the instruction.

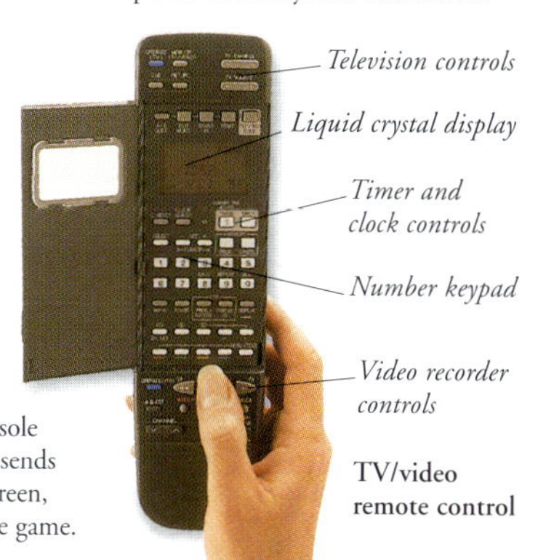

Television controls

Liquid crystal display

Timer and clock controls

Number keypad

Video recorder controls

TV/video remote control

FIND OUT MORE
Computers · Electricity · Elements · Information Technology · Metals · Telecommunications · Telephones · Video

ELEMENTS

AN ELEMENT IS a substance composed of only one type of atom. Elements are the most basic substances in the Universe and cannot be split into anything simpler. There are 109 elements – 91 of which occur naturally, and 18 of which can be made artificially. All life on Earth is based on the element carbon, which is vital to the functioning of living cells. Oxygen is the most plentiful element on Earth. It occurs in air, water, and even rocks.

Elements in nature

Only a few of the naturally occurring elements can be found in their pure state. Most elements combine, or react, with other elements to form more complex substances called compounds. Pure gold can be mined directly from the ground because it is unreactive – that is, it does not readily form compounds.

Quartz rock is a compound of the elements silicon and oxygen.

Pure gold.

Gold veins in quartz rock

Groups of elements

Just as the members of a human family share the same characteristics, there are "families" of elements that have similar properties. An element's chemical properties are determined by the structure of its atoms. Elements in the same group have similar atomic structures.

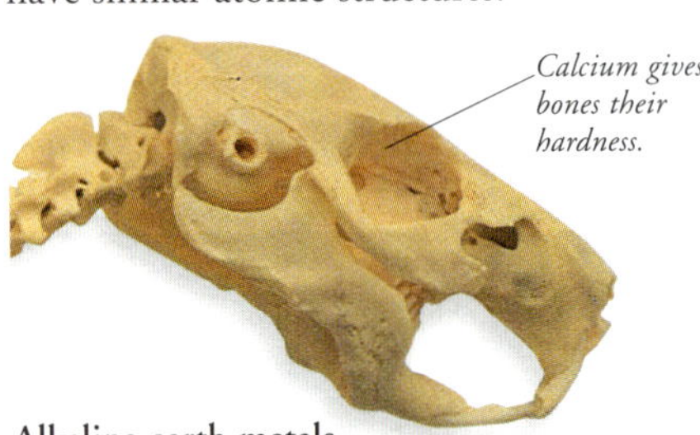

Calcium gives bones their hardness.

Alkaline-earth metals

Calcium and magnesium belong to the group of elements called the alkaline-earth metals. They are so named because they form alkaline solutions in water, and their compounds occur widely in nature. Calcium, for example, occurs in sea shells, bones, teeth, milk, and chalk. Magnesium occurs in the substance chlorophyll, which plants use to make food by photosynthesis.

Iodine Bromine Chlorine

Halogens

Swimming pools smell the way they do because the halogen chlorine is put in the water to kill germs. Compounds of fluorine, another halogen, are put in water and toothpaste to prevent tooth decay. The halogens, which also include iodine, bromine, and astatine, are all strong-smelling, highly reactive non-metals.

Alkali metals

Potassium (which is used in fertilizers) and sodium (which occurs in salt) are both alkali metals. All the elements in this group are soft, extremely reactive metals. They react violently or even explosively with water to form alkaline solutions.

Reaction of potassium in water

Iron compounds are often red, black, or brown.

Iron sulphide

Iron carbide

Iron oxide

Coloured compounds of iron

Transition metals

The transition metals are a large group of hard, dense elements that conduct electricity and heat well, form coloured compounds, and some of which (iron, cobalt, and nickel) are magnetic. Other transition metals include copper, gold, chromium, titanium, platinum, and tungsten.

Noble gases

Multi-coloured street signs often contain noble gases, because each of these gases glows a different colour when electricity flows through it. Neon, for example, glows red, helium yellow, and argon blue. The noble gases are unreactive non-metals that rarely form compounds.

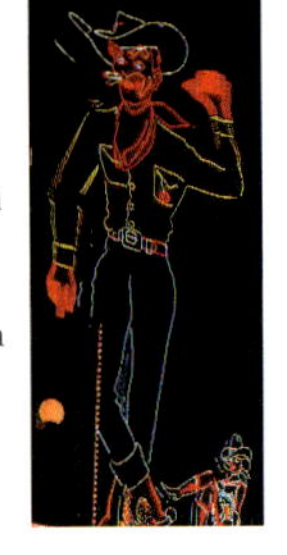

Allotropes

It may seem difficult to believe, but hard, sparkling diamond is made of the same types of atoms as soft, black graphite. Diamond and graphite are allotropes of carbon, meaning that they are different physical forms of the same element. Their atoms link up in different ways to make them look and behave differently.

Graphite pencil

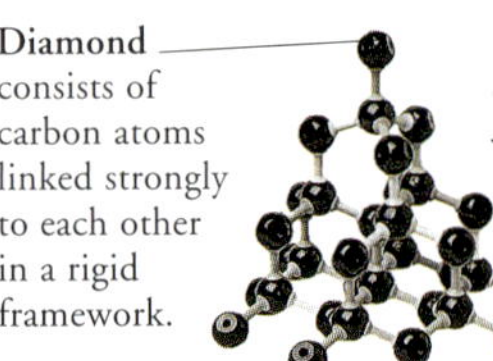

Diamond consists of carbon atoms linked strongly to each other in a rigid framework.

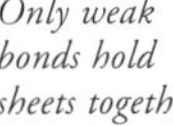

Only weak bonds hold sheets together.

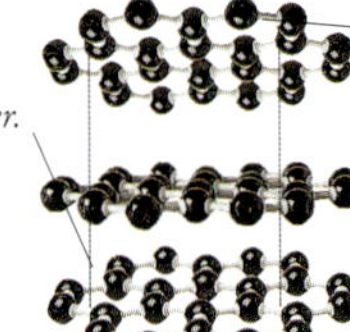

Graphite is made up of sheets of carbon atoms that can slide over each other easily.

Artificial elements

New elements can be created by bombarding existing elements with high-speed subatomic particles in a device called a particle accelerator. Since 1937, scientists have made 18 new elements, some of which only exist for a few millionths of a second.

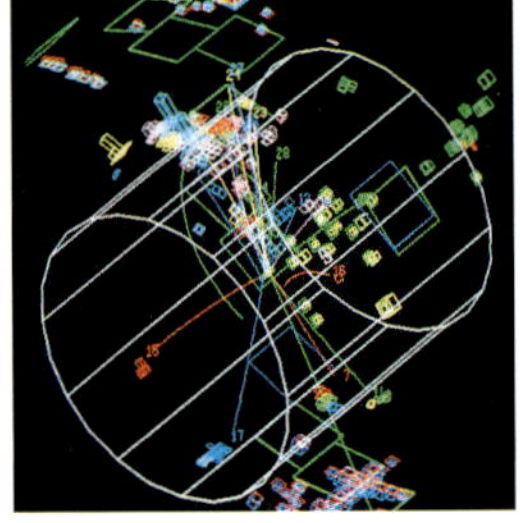

Computer image of a particle accelerator collision

Hydrogen

The element hydrogen makes up 90 per cent of all the matter in the Universe. It was the first element to form when the Universe was created in the explosion known as the Big Bang. Hydrogen is a tasteless, colourless, odourless, non-toxic gas. It is the simplest of all the elements, with atoms containing just one proton orbited by a single electron. Hydrogen gives acids their acidic properties.

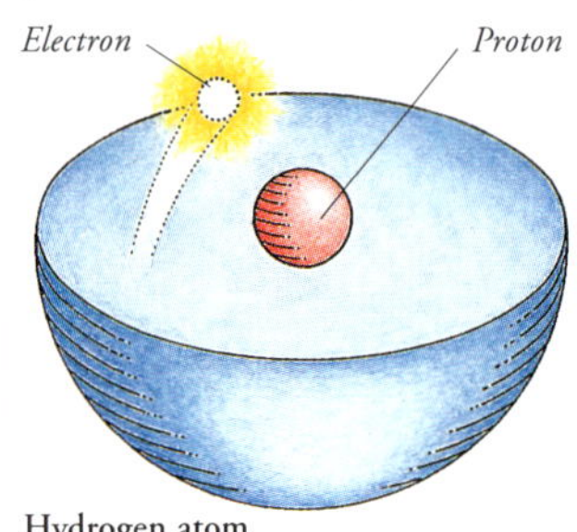

Hydrogen atom

Dmitri Mendeleyev

In 1869, the Russian chemist Dmitri Mendeleyev (1834–1907) devised a chart called the periodic table, which classified the 63 elements then known into different groups. He used the table to predict the existence of three new elements, all of which were discovered a few years later.

FIND OUT MORE: ACIDS AND ALKALIS · AIR · ATOMS AND MOLECULES · BIG BANG · MATTER · METALS · MIXTURES AND COMPOUNDS · SKELETON · TEETH AND JAWS

ELEPHANTS

THE AFRICAN AND ASIAN elephants are the only two living species of a once much larger family that was found on every continent. The African elephant is the largest land mammal, but despite its size and power it is a gentle creature. Elephants are highly intelligent, very sociable animals, that live in close family units. The African and Asian elephants are descended from different ancestors; the Asian elephant is more closely related to the mammoth than to the African elephant.

Features of an elephant

Everything about an elephant is oversized. Its most conspicuous feature is the long flexible trunk – an elongation of the nose. The huge tusks are overgrown incisor teeth. Besides hearing, the large ears are used as a fan to cool the elephant. They also make the animal appear larger than it really is, and spreading the ears helps intimidate a rival or a potential enemy. Soft fatty cushions on the underside of the feet spread as the elephant walks.

Elephant using tusks to dig into ground.

Tusks

A tusk is a specialized type of tooth, growing from either side of the upper jaw. Tusks are used mainly as tools and weapons. The heaviest pair of tusks ever recorded weighed 102 kg (225 lb) and 109 kg (240 lb). The longest pair measured 3.35 m (11 ft) and 3.5 m (11 ft 5 in) in length.

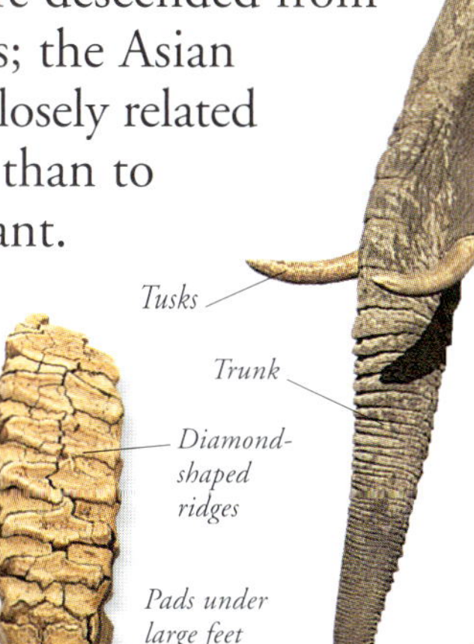

Large ears

Tusks

Trunk

Diamond-shaped ridges

Pads under large feet expand when trodden on.

Tail

Teeth

The elephant has only four teeth, one in each quarter of the jaw. Each tooth is about 30 cm (12 in) long. As one wears down, another pushes in from behind. This can happen only six times, after which the supply of teeth is exhausted. Without teeth, the elephant can no longer eat, so dies of starvation.

Skin

The skin is very wrinkled. Deep crevices increase the surface area of the skin, and allow greater heat loss. The crevices also help to trap water which then takes longer to evaporate, and helps to keep the elephant cooler for longer.

Trunk

The elephant uses its trunk to feed.

Fingers are used to hold objects.

The elephant's trunk is highly flexible and serves much the same functions as a human arm and hand. It combines great strength with delicacy, and is so versatile that it can pluck a single leaf as easily as it can lift a heavy log. Because the elephant has a trunk it does not need to lower its head while feeding, thus allowing it to remain alert. The trunk also allows the elephant to reach high above its head to browse on leaves that are out of most other animals' reach.

Nostrils

Located at the tip of the trunk, the elephant's nostrils can be raised high above its head, like a periscope, and turned in any direction to pick up traces of scent carried on the wind. The elephant relies on its sense of smell more than its other senses. While swimming, the trunk may be lifted above the surface of the water, and used as a snorkel if the elephant gets out of its depth.

Picking up scent on the wind

Fingers

As well as the nostrils, the tip of the trunk has fleshy "fingers". The African species has two opposing fingers, but the Asian elephant has only one which it uses to grip against the wide underside of the trunk. Fingers enable the elephant to perform precise movements and pick up very small objects.

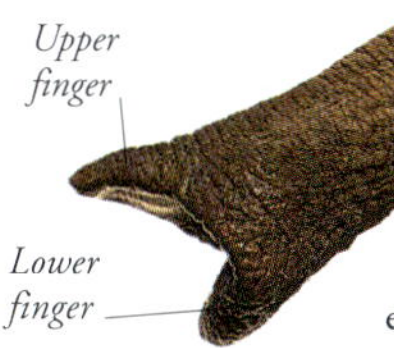

Upper finger

Lower finger

Fingers of the African elephant trunk

Ivory trade

The elephant's only enemy is humans, who kill them for their tusks. In recent years, the demand for ivory has led to killing on a vast scale. From 1979 to 1989, the number of elephants in Africa was reduced from 1.3 million to 609,000.

Ivory is made into carvings and trinkets.

Types of elephant

Asian elephant

The Asian elephant, found in forests in India and south-eastern Asia, has been domesticated for at least 2,500 years. It is used for ceremonial purposes and forestry work. Of the 34,000–56,000 elephants remaining in Asia, 10,000 are working animals.

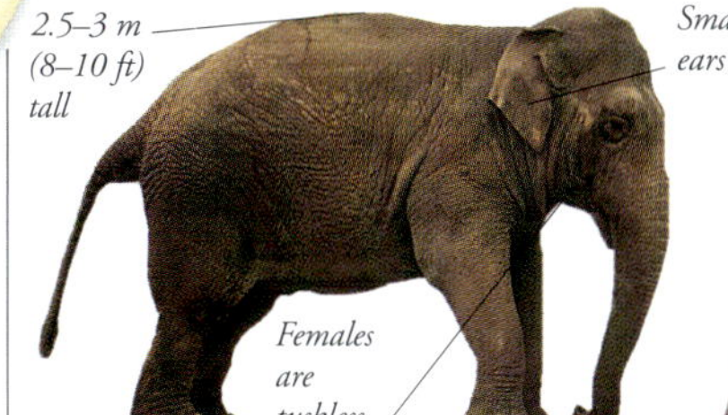

2.5–3 m (8–10 ft) tall

Small ears

Females are tuskless.

African bush elephant

The African bush elephant lives in open country and woodland in Africa south of the Sahara. It is larger, with much larger ears and a more concave back than the Asian elephant. Both males and females have tusks. Unlike the Asian elephant, it has never been domesticated.

4 m (13 ft) tall

Large ears

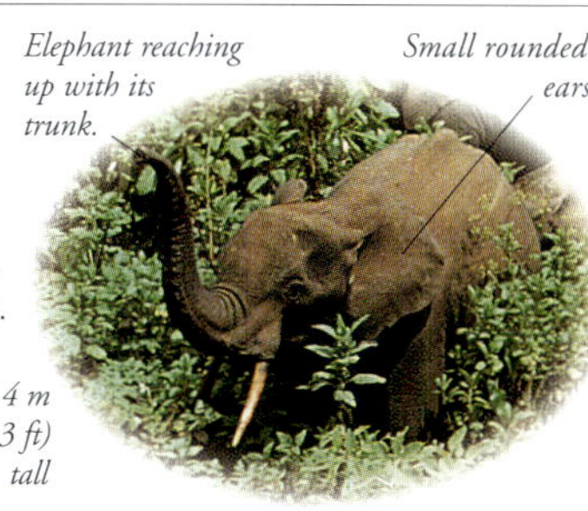

Elephant reaching up with its trunk.

Small rounded ears

African forest elephant

The forest elephant is a smaller subspecies of the African bush elephant, with smaller, more rounded ears. It does not need such large ears to help it keep cool, as it lives in the tropical rainforests of the Congo basin in equatorial Africa. Its tusks are slender and downward pointing.

E

Family group

The elephant's social organization is based upon a group of 10–12 females and their calves, led by a mature female. Harmonious relationships often develop between individual members of the group. Friendships can last for decades as elephants often live for up to 80 years. Elephants show great affection for their young, but discipline is strong, and any lapse of acceptable behaviour is dealt with firmly. Family groups often seek shade during the heat of the day, preferring to feed and drink in the cool of the evening. Elephants browse on leaves and shoots, but they also eat grass. They spend about 18 hours a day feeding, to satisfy their huge appetites.

Herd gathering

Separate family groups associate closely with each other. They often live only a few hundred metres apart, constantly coming together and drifting apart again. Occasionally, many family groups congregate in an exceptionally large herd of more than a thousand animals.

Young

Females normally conceive every four years and give birth to a single calf after 22 months' gestation. This is the longest gestation period of any animal. The newborn calf stands about 84 cm (33 in) high. Other calves from previous matings remain with their mother after the new calf is born. The older calves help to take care of their younger siblings.

Matriarch

Leadership of the family unit rests with the oldest and most experienced female, the matriarch, who is usually the mother or grandmother of the whole group. Each member of the group knows its position in the hierarchy and respects matriarchal authority without question.

Water holes

Elephants like to drink every day. They also enjoy bathing and spraying themselves with water. As the dry season advances, food and water become scarce, and they may have to walk up to 80 km (50 miles) between watering and feeding grounds. They also dig holes in some riverbeds to reach water below the surface, thereby providing water for other animals.

Secretion shows bull is in musth.

Bulls

Only immature bull calves are allowed in the family group; as soon as the bulls reach maturity they are expelled. They live alone or in small bachelor groups. Mature bulls briefly rejoin the herd when any of the cows are ready for mating.

Musth

By 25 years of age, bulls come into musth once a year. Musth is a period of aggressive behaviour where a bull picks fights with other bulls searching for a female ready to mate. A thick secretion from the temporal gland indicates he is in musth.

Fighting

Young bulls often have mock battles to test each other's strength. They are usually harmless affairs where they clash tusks and grapple with each other's trunks. Older bulls, especially those in musth, may sometimes fight in defence of territory or to establish dominance.

Young bulls sparring

Threat displays

Differences between elephants are generally resolved peacefully. Displeasure is indicated by means of a threat display. This involves head-shaking, ear-spreading, trunk-twirling, and foot-shuffling. If this fails to deter, the elephant may make a full-scale charge. This is a rare event where the elephant covers ground at rapid speed, with its trunk raised and ears outstretched, while trumpeting furiously. Threat charges are rarely carried through; the elephant usually halts or turns at the last moment.

Ears spread wide to intimidate an enemy

Communication

Touch is an important way of communicating in elephant society. When elephants meet, they greet each other by entwining trunks and touching each other's face and body. At rest, they often stand together, head to head. If a young calf misbehaves, its mother may actually use her trunk to smack it. When a calf is frightened, other elephants help to calm it by standing close, and caressing it with their trunks.

Elephants standing face to face and touching each others' heads and trunks.

Rumbling

Elephants maintain contact by means of rumbling sounds from the throat, back of the nose, and trunk. A sudden cessation of rumbling warns the herd of possible danger. Elephants are also capable of communicating over substantial distances, by low-frequency sounds which humans cannot hear.

African elephant

Scientific name *Loxodonta africana*

Order Proboscidea

Family Elephantidae

Distribution Africa south of the Sahara

Habitat Open savannahs and woodlands

Diet Grasses, leaves, shoots, twigs, and other browse

Size Height at shoulder: 4 m (13 ft); weight: 6.1 tonnes (6 tons)

Lifespan 70–80 years

FIND OUT MORE

African Wildlife | Animal Behaviour | Asian Wildlife | Conservation | Ecology and Ecosystems | Grassland Wildlife | Mammals | Rainforest Wildlife

ELIZABETH I

FOR 45 YEARS from 1558–1603, a truly remarkable woman governed England. By force of personality and political skill, Queen Elizabeth I united her divided country and presided over a glorious period in the arts and culture. Yet she had to struggle all her life: her mother died when she was only three, her half-sister, Mary, put her in prison and, as an adult, she was a single woman in a world dominated by men. But Elizabeth overcame every adversity, and when she died in 1603, she left England one of the most prosperous and powerful nations in Europe.

Elizabeth I's accession to the throne, at the age of 25

Early life

Elizabeth was the daughter of Henry VIII (r.1509–47) and his second wife, Anne Boleyn. She was born in Greenwich Palace on 7 September, 1533. Elizabeth's mother was executed for treason when Elizabeth was just three years old. The future queen was imprisoned briefly while her Catholic half-sister Mary was crowned queen. Elizabeth took the throne on 17 November, 1558, after Mary's death.

Church and State

Elizabeth's father Henry VIII broke with the Roman Catholic Church in 1534, establishing the Protestant Church of England. Her half-sister Mary I (r.1553–58) tried to return England to Catholicism, but Elizabeth introduced the Anglican faith, as a compromise between Catholicism and extreme Protestantism.

William Cecil

Cecil, later Lord Burghley, served Elizabeth first as her Chief Secretary of State and, after 1572, as Lord Treasurer. He introduced many reforms and was an able adviser to the queen. He died in 1598, and his son became chief minister.

Mary, Queen of Scots

Mary was Elizabeth's heir, but also a Catholic. She became the centre of plots against Elizabeth, notably one led by Mary's page Anthony Babington. Elizabeth reluctantly had Mary tried and executed for treason in 1587.

Spanish Armada

As leader of Catholic Europe, Philip II of Spain, husband of Elizabeth's half-sister Mary, was a threat to Protestant England and encouraged plots against the queen. After the execution of Mary, Queen of Scots, Philip decided to invade England. In 1588, he sent a huge Armada of 130 ships carrying 20,000 soldiers. Harried by English ships, attacked in the English Channel, and wrecked by severe storms, the Armada was forced to return, in defeat, to Spain.

English fire ships are sent to meet the Spanish fleet.

Spanish ships escape towards the North.

Francis Drake

Between 1577 and 1580, in his ship the *Golden Hind*, Francis Drake became the first Englishman to sail around the world. He delayed preparations for the Spanish Armada by attacking the fleet while it was at anchor in Cadiz Harbour in 1587, and played an important part in its defeat the following year. He continued to attack Spanish shipping until his death off the coast of Panama in 1596.

Phoenix emblem

Elizabeth created a strong public image of herself by adopting the phoenix as her emblem. The "Phoenix Jewel", dated around 1574, shows a bust of Elizabeth, with a reverse image of the mythical phoenix rising from flames.

The famous "Phoenix Jewel"

Virgin Queen

Elizabeth spent her life surrounded by suitors, yet she never married. Powerful foreign monarchs courted Elizabeth throughout her life, eager for a stake in her flourishing kingdom, but she played her suitors off against each other for political gains. Elizabeth gloried in her role as the Virgin Queen, using it to create a national self-confidence that fuelled a flowering of the arts, distinguished by William Shakespeare, the poet Edmund Spenser, and composers such as Thomas Tallis.

Elizabeth stands on a map of her kingdom.

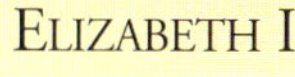

ELIZABETH I

1533 Born in Greenwich Palace near London, England.

1536 Elizabeth's mother, Anne Boleyn, executed for treason.

1554 Elizabeth put under house arrest by half-sister, Mary.

1558 Succeeds to the throne; appoints William Cecil as Secretary of State and Matthew Parker as Archbishop of Canterbury.

1559 Act of Supremacy makes her head of Anglican Church.

1588 Spanish Armada defeated.

1603 Dies in Richmond Palace.

FIND OUT MORE

CHRISTIANITY · DRAMA · HOUSES AND HOMES · REFORMATION · SHAKESPEARE, WILLIAM · SPAIN, HISTORY OF · THEATRES · UNITED KINGDOM, HISTORY OF

E

EMPIRES

A LARGE SUPER-STATE under a single ruler is called an empire. There have been many different empires through history, from the ancient Roman Empire to the great empire of the Incas in Peru. The largest ever was the British Empire. Most empires have an army, to conquer territory and suppress revolts, and a civil service to carry out the day-to-day running of the empire and collect taxes. No empire lasts for ever – though the effect on the host country may be permanent – and empires perish for many reasons, including internal rebellion, economic decline, or the sheer difficulty of uniting many peoples under one leader.

Ottoman sword and scabbard

Growth of empires

Empires grow because ruling powers want extra income from trade or taxes, or they may have territorial ambitions. Sometimes they may want to spread a religion. Would-be empires always need a strong army.

Ottoman Empire

The Ottoman Turks expanded their empire by military might. At their height in the 17th century, they dominated the Mediterranean coast from present-day Greece to Tunisia.

Imperial cross

Holy Roman Empire

Based in Germany, the leaders of this empire saw themselves as heirs to the Roman emperors. The emperors wanted to wield religious power over all western Christians, and to exert political power over the other European rulers, such as the German and Italian princes.

British Empire

The largest empire the world has ever seen had its beginnings in the 18th and early 19th centuries, when Britain acquired Australia, Canada, and a range of territories from Honduras to Hong Kong. The "jewel in the crown" of the empire was India, which Britain dominated through the East India Company. Queen Victoria (r.1837–1901) took the title Empress of India in 1876. The British Empire had a lasting influence on its territories – for both good and bad. British-style administration provided a model for local civil servants when territories gained independence. On the other hand, the British exploited local labour forces on a massive scale.

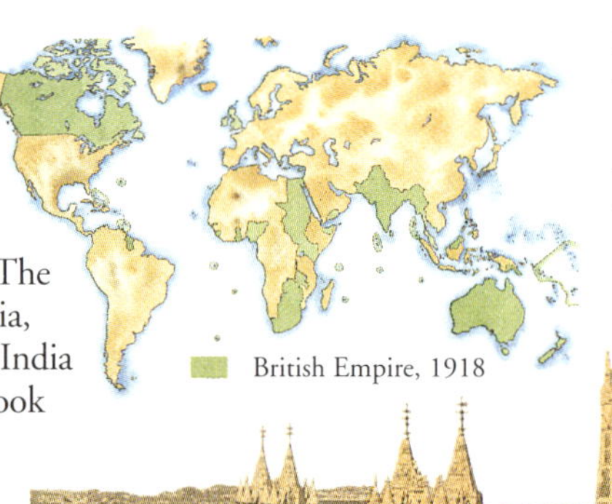

Extent of the empire

After winning the Napoleonic Wars, and the decline of the older empires of Spain, Portugal, and the Netherlands, Britain was clearly one of the world's strongest countries. As the 19th century wore on, the already vast British Empire added parts of Africa and South-east Asia. By 1918, the empire had reached its peak.

Victoria Station, Bombay, India

Gordon of Khartoum

In 1884, two years after Egypt became part of the empire, General Charles Gordon (1833–85) came to the Sudan to aid Egyptians defending their garrisons against a local revolt. Gordon was cut off in the city of Khartoum and withstood a 10-month siege, but was finally killed. There was outcry that a relief force had not been sent soon enough to save Gordon, and he became a hero of the empire.

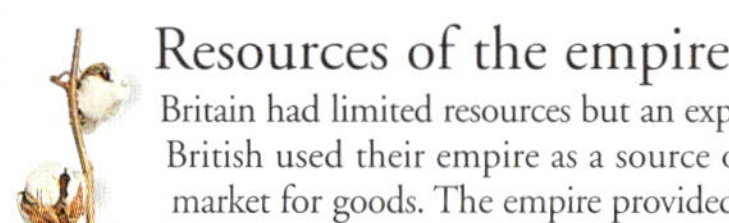

Resources of the empire

Britain had limited resources but an expanding industry, so the British used their empire as a source of raw materials, and a market for goods. The empire provided raw materials, such as cotton, gemstones, and hard wood, and raw materials included tea, rubber, tin, copper, and wool.

Cotton **Emerald** **Timber**

Public works

The British made the major towns of the empire as similar to British cities as possible. They sent British engineers and architects all over the world to build government headquarters, churches, railway stations, art galleries, and public buildings. Former imperial cities, such as Bombay, still have Victorian-era administration and transport centres.

Timeline

509 BC–AD 476 Roman Empire dominates much of Europe, western Asia, and northern Africa.

221–206 BC Qin emperor unites China.

321–187 BC Mauryans rule much of India.

395–1453 Byzantine Empire established in the eastern territory of the Roman Empire.

962–1806 Holy Roman Empire dominates central Europe.

1206–1405 Mongols create an empire, including most of Asia.

1345–1521 Aztec emperors hold power in Mexico.

Conquistadore's helmet

1521–1825 Spain builds large empire in southern America.

1580–1931 British Empire increases in size.

1930s British Empire starts to decline. By the 1940s, territories are claiming independence.

Imperialism

The economic domination of Asia, North America, and Africa by Europe, the United States, and Russia from the 17th century is known as modern imperialism. Ancient imperialism peaked with the Roman Empire.

The bear, symbol of Russia, 1888

FIND OUT MORE

BYZANTINE EMPIRE · HOLY ROMAN EMPIRE · ISLAMIC EMPIRE · OTTOMAN EMPIRE · PERSIAN EMPIRES · ROMAN EMPIRE

ENERGY

WE RELY ON THE ENERGY stored in food to keep us alive and on the energy locked within fuels to drive our machines and industries. Energy is the ability to make things happen, whether it is moving something, heating it up, or changing it in some way. Energy exists in many different forms, including electricity, sound, heat, and light.

Weights gain potential energy.

When this woman lifts the weights, she is doing work.

Her power is how long it takes her to do the work.

Work

When a force moves an object, energy changes from one form to another and work is the result. This woman does work as she lifts weights. The force she applies converts the kinetic energy of her moving arms into the potential energy of the raised weights. Multiplying the force by the distance through which the object moves gives the amount of work done.

Types of energy

All energy is either kinetic or potential. Kinetic energy is the energy of moving objects, while potential energy is energy that is stored, ready for use. Energy is measured in units called joules (J).

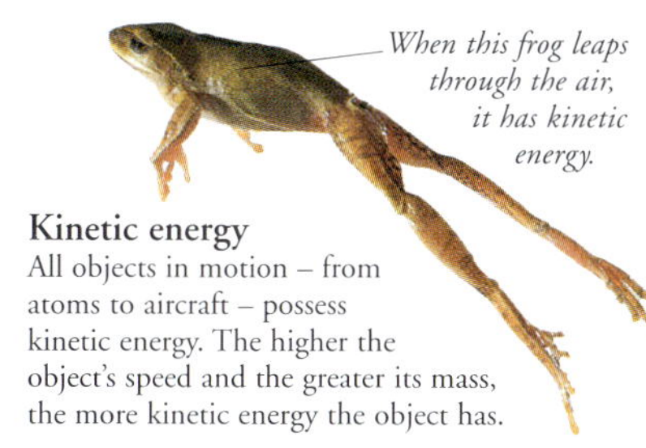

When this frog leaps through the air, it has kinetic energy.

Kinetic energy

All objects in motion – from atoms to aircraft – possess kinetic energy. The higher the object's speed and the greater its mass, the more kinetic energy the object has.

Potential energy

An object may gain potential energy if its position or condition alters. A bungee-jumper standing on top of a bridge has potential energy – that is, the potential to fall back to Earth. When he jumps, his bungee rope gains potential energy as it stretches, because it has the potential to pull him back up again.

The jumper's potential energy changes to kinetic energy as he falls.

500 g (1.1 lb) peas

90 g (3 oz) beef

50 g (1.8 oz) sugar

500 g (1.1 lb) peeled oranges

30 g (1 oz) butter

50 g (1.8 oz) cheese

Chemical energy

Foods and fuels contain energy stored within chemical compounds. This is a type of potential energy called chemical energy. Some foods store more energy than others. All the foods above contain the same amount of energy, but you would have to eat 500 g (1.1 lb) of peas to get as much energy as you would from just 30 g (1 oz) of butter.

Power

The rate at which work is done and energy changed from one form to another is called power. Power is measured in watts (W), and is calculated by dividing the work done by the time taken to do it.

100 W fan

1,000 W iron

Electrical power

Every electrical appliance is given a power rating. If a fan has a power rating of 100 W, it shows that the fan converts 100 J of electrical energy into kinetic energy each second. Similarly, a 1,000 W iron changes electricity into heat at the rate of 1,000 J per second.

Both bulbs give out the same light.

60 W bulb (incandescent)

15 W bulb (fluorescent)

Fluorescent bulb uses less electricity.

Efficiency

Out of every 100 J of electrical energy used by a 60 W incandescent bulb, only 10 J are changed into light; the rest are lost as heat. The bulb has an efficiency of 10%. A 15 W fluorescent bulb is 40% efficient. It gives the same light using a quarter of the electricity.

Energy transfer

The Law of Conservation of Energy says that energy is always conserved – that is, it can be neither created nor destroyed. This law means that when objects gain or lose energy, the energy simply transfers from place to place, or changes into a different form.

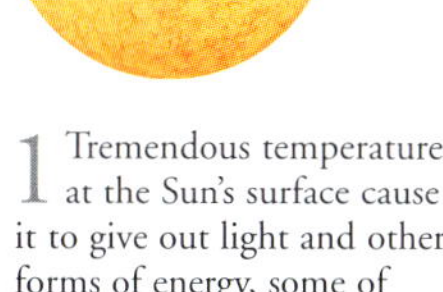

Harvested wheat

Bread is made from wheat.

Friction occurs between brake and wheel.

1 Tremendous temperatures at the Sun's surface cause it to give out light and other forms of energy, some of which reach the Earth.

2 When sunlight falls on plants, some of the light energy transfers to the plants by a process called photosynthesis. It is stored as chemical energy.

3 Eating plant-based food, such as bread, enables you to break down the food. This releases the chemical energy and transfers it to your body.

4 Riding a bicycle changes the chemical energy into kinetic energy. If you brake, friction changes this energy into heat as you slow down.

James Joule

The unit of energy, the joule, is named after the English physicist James Joule (1818–89), who helped to develop the Law of Conservation of Energy. Joule noticed that if he rotated a set of paddles in water, the water soon became warm. He realized that the work of turning the paddles changed their kinetic energy into heat, proving that heat is a form of energy.

Timeline

1829 French physicist Gustave Coriolis introduces the term "kinetic energy".

1843 James Joule's experiments show how heat, work, and power are related.

1847 Joule and German physicists Hermann von Helmholtz and Julius Meyer independently state the Law of Conservation of Energy.

1853 Scottish scientist William Rankine devises the concept of "potential energy".

1881 The world's first electricity-generating power station opens in Surrey, UK.

1884 Irish engineer Charles Parsons invents the steam turbine.

Parsons' turbine

1905 German physicist Albert Einstein suggests that matter is a form of energy, and vice versa.

1980s Declining fossil fuel reserves and pollution bring calls for machines and industries to be more energy efficient.

E

Power station

Most of the energy used in homes, offices, and factories is electricity produced by power stations. Inside a coal- or oil-fired power station, chemical energy stored within fuel turns into heat energy as the fuel burns in a furnace. The heat is used to boil water into steam, which drives turbines linked to electricity generators. The electricity reaches consumers via a network of cables called a grid.

Model of a coal-fired power station

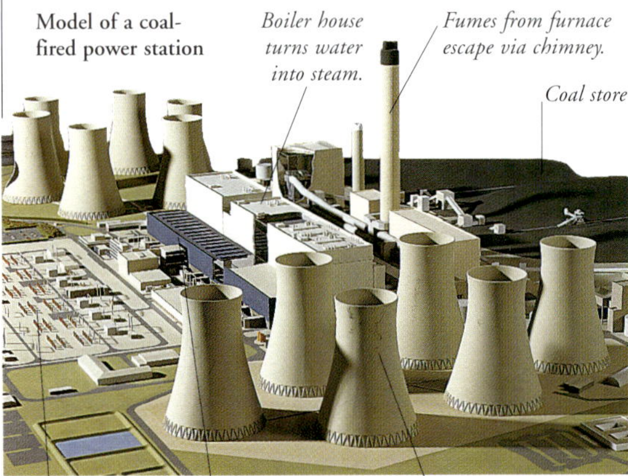

Boiler house turns water into steam.

Fumes from furnace escape via chimney.

Coal store

Connections to electricity grid

The turbine house contains the turbines and generators.

Cooling towers turn steam from the boiler back into water.

The turbine blades revolve about 3,000 times each minute.

The generator uses the motion of the turbine to produce electricity.

Turbine-generator unit in a coal-fired power station

Turbine

A turbine is a machine powered by the force of moving liquid or gas. It consists of a set of angled blades mounted on a shaft. In a power station, jets of high-pressure steam strike the turbine blades and make them revolve at high speed. The turbine shaft is connected to an electricity generator. As the shaft spins, it turns an electromagnet inside the generator, producing an electric current.

Renewable energy

Energy that is produced without permanently using up the Earth's limited resources is called renewable energy. Apart from biomass fuels, which produce smoke and other fumes when burned, renewable energy sources are pollution-free, because they harness the energy of natural phenomena such as winds and waves. As the Earth's fossil fuel reserves are gradually used up, people will have to rely much more on renewable energy sources.

Solar power

Electricity produced from sunlight is called solar power. A "solar furnace" uses a vast bank of mirrors to focus sunlight on to water. The water boils into steam, which drives turbines and generators.

Geothermal power

Below the Earth's surface, water is turned into steam by geothermal energy – that is, the energy of hot, molten rocks. By drilling a well, this steam can be harnessed to drive generators. Electricity produced in this way is called geothermal power.

Wind power

A wind turbine is a tall tower with propeller-like blades that converts the kinetic energy of the wind into electricity. As the wind blows, the turbine's blades rotate and drive a small generator. A group of wind turbines is called a wind farm.

Biomass fuels

Plant material is called biomass. Millions of people around the world burn peat, wood, animal dung, and other biomass fuels to heat and light their homes, and to cook food. Burning biomass fuels releases chemical energy stored within the plant material.

Hydroelectric power

A hydroelectric power station converts the kinetic energy of falling water into electricity. The power station sits under a dam at the end of a reservoir. Inside the power station, turbines and generators are driven by water rushing down with tremendous force from the reservoir above.

Wave power

Towers such as the one above stand in coastal waters and use the movement of the ocean's waves to produce electricity. As the waves rise and fall, they push a column of air inside the tower up and down. The to-and-fro motion of the air turns a turbine and drives a generator.

Tidal barrage

At high and low tides, huge amounts of water move up and down river estuaries. A tidal barrage is a dam across an estuary. As the tides come in and go out, some water is allowed to pass through tunnels in the dam. The tidal flow drives electricity generators built into the dam.

Fossil fuels

Coal, oil, and natural gas are called fossil fuels, because they formed underground over millions of years from the fossilized remains of plants and animals. The Earth has limited supplies of these fuels, which cannot be replenished once exhausted.

Natural gas is made up of methane and small amounts of other gases.

Petrol, diesel, and many other fuels are made from oil.

Coal consists chiefly of the element carbon.

Natural gas Oil Coal

Charles Parsons

The engineer Charles Parsons (1854–1931) was born in London, England, of Irish parents. He is best known for inventing the steam turbine in 1884. Power stations around the world still use steam turbines based on Parson's designs. In 1897, his boat *Turbinia* became the first to use a steam turbine to power its propellers.

World energy use

Around 90 per cent of all the energy used comes from fossil fuels, which give out a lot of energy when burned, but release polluting gases into the air. Nuclear power is an alternative to fossil fuels, but produces dangerous radioactive waste. Hydroelectric power is the only form of renewable energy that is used in any significant amount.

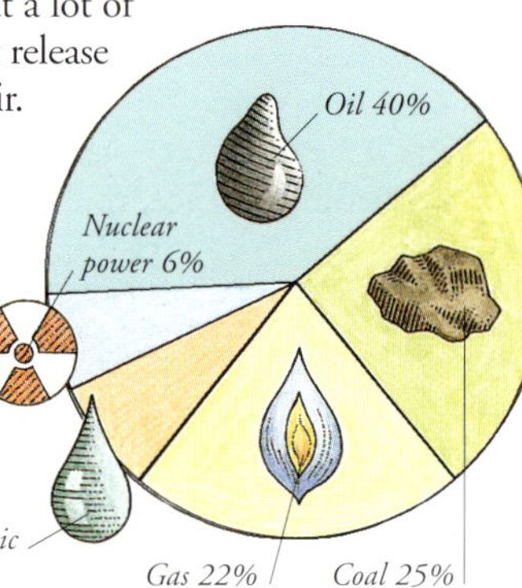

FIND OUT MORE

COAL | ELECTRICITY | FOOD | HEAT AND TEMPERATURE | LIGHT | NUCLEAR POWER | OIL | SOUND | X-RAYS AND THE ELECTROMAGNETIC SPECTRUM

ENGINES AND MOTORS

EVERY MACHINE THAT MOVES OR HAS moving parts needs an engine or a motor to make it work. A motor is a machine that converts some form of energy, such as fuel or electricity, into motion. An engine is a form of motor. Engines and motors, both huge and tiny, are everywhere – in vehicles from motor cycles to airliners and railway locomotives, and in appliances around the house, in industrial machines, and in power stations.

Early engines

The first engines were developed in the middle of the 18th century, and were steam powered. During the 19th century, a new form of engine was developed: the internal combustion engine, which was lighter and had more practical uses than its predecessor.

Early four-cylinder petrol engine

Modern engines

Fuel efficiency, plenty of power for its low weight, and little need for maintenance are the hallmarks of the modern car engine. Many engines have electronic components that increase their fuel efficiency further.

Internal combustion engine
Most cars are fitted with internal combustion engines – so-called because they combust, or burn, fuel inside a cylinder. The power this combustion produces is harnessed by pistons and used to power the engine.

Exterior of internal combustion engine

Sectioned view of a petrol-fuelled internal combustion engine

Camshaft controls the opening and closing of the valves. There are separate camshafts for fuel inlet and exhaust valves.

Timing belt drives the camshaft.

Spark plug

Combustion chamber is where fuel burns to force the piston down.

Distributor feeds a spark of electricity to each cylinder at the right moment, to start the fuel burning.

Valves let fresh fuel into each cylinder, and spent gases out.

Valve assembly

Exhaust manifold channels waste gases and heat to exhaust pipe.

Cylinder and piston

Water pump pulley

Oil filter

Sump reservoir for lubricating oil

The pistons slide up and down in the cylinders, providing the driving force that keeps the engine running. The number of cylinders in an engine varies; there are usually at least four, and sometimes more.

Crankshaft turns the wheels via the clutch and gearbox. Connecting rods turn the up-and-down motion of the pistons into the circular motion of the crankshaft.

Lubricating oil is pumped around the engine, continuously covering the moving parts with a thin film of oil that stops them rubbing together and wearing out.

How engines work

This sequence of diagrams shows what happens in one cylinder of a petrol engine while the engine is running. During the sequence, the piston goes down, up, down, and up again. This is called a four-stroke cycle. The cycle is repeated over and over again – up to 50 times a second when the engine is turning at high speed. In an engine with more than one cylinder, the cylinders fire one after the other to provide continuous power.

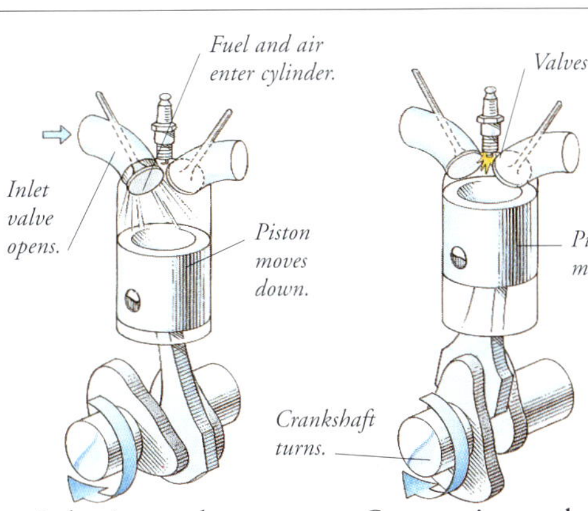

Induction stroke
The piston moves down, and the inlet valve opens. A mixture of fuel and air is sucked into the cylinder.

Compression stroke
The valve closes. The piston moves up again, squeezing the fuel and air into the top of the cylinder.

Valves closed

Spark plug

Explosion forces piston down.

Power stroke
The spark plug flares and ignites the fuel which explodes, pushing the piston back down.

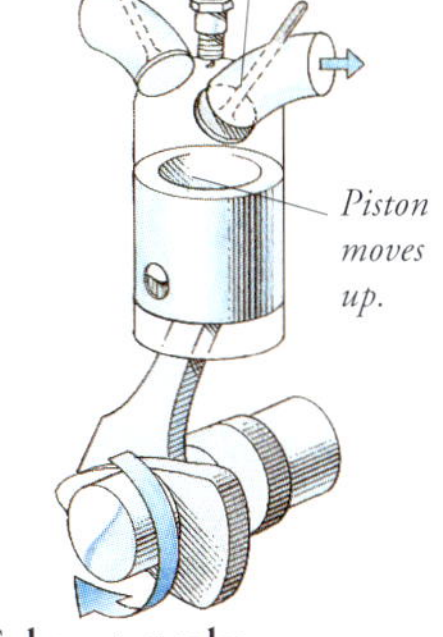

Exhaust stroke
The piston moves up, pushing waste gases out of the cylinder. The exhaust valve opens to let exhaust gases out.

E

Eight-cylinder diesel truck engine

Diesel engine

A diesel engine is a four-stroke engine without spark plugs. The engine's cylinder has a piston, which rises and falls, squashing the fuel-and-air mixture in the cylinder into a tiny space. The mixture gets so hot, it explodes.

Using diesels

Diesel engines are very fuel-efficient. They are used for driving electricity generators, and in vehicles that need to keep going for long periods without refuelling, such as lorries, taxis, trains, ships, and boats. Many modern cars are also fitted with diesel engines.

Steam engine

The pistons of a steam engine are moved up and down in their cylinders by steam under high pressure. The pistons are connected to rods that turn the wheels. The steam is made outside the cylinders by heating water in a coal-fired boiler, which is why steam engines are called external combustion engines.

Using steam

Until the middle of the 1900s, most railway locomotives and ships were powered by steam engines. Steam also drove many early trucks and buses. The first steam engines were used for pumping flood water out of mines, and to work industrial machines.

Steam engine

Solar power

Petroleum and coal are fossil fuels, formed from decayed prehistoric organisms. They are expensive to produce, and create harmful gases when they burn. Solar energy is energy from the Sun. It can be used to heat houses, run air conditioning, and to generate electricity to power lightweight vehicles.

Solar panels

Sunlight can be turned into electricity by solar panels. These are made from many photovoltaic cells. The bigger the area of photovoltaic cells, and the brighter the sunlight, the larger the electric current the solar panel will produce.

Solar-powered car

Gas turbine engines

In a gas turbine, burning fuel makes a stream of hot gas that spins a set of turbine blades very fast. A shaft attached to the turbine drives a compressor that sucks air into the engine so the fuel burns.

Jet engine

High-speed aircraft have a type of turbine called a turbojet or turbofan. The stream of hot air and gases created in the engine turns the turbine, then shoots out of the back of the engine, pushing the aircraft forwards.

Turboshaft engine

Some turbine engines make ship or aircraft propellers spin. The spinning turbine turns a shaft connected to the propeller. Large hovercraft have turboshaft engines to create their air cushion and to drive their propellers. Large helicopters also have turboshaft engines to turn their rotors.

SR.N4 ferry hovercraft

Electric motors

An electric motor produces movement from electricity. Inside it are electromagnets – wire coils that become magnets when an electric current flows through them. The electromagnets are turned on and off in sequence to pull a magnetic shaft around and around. Motors are used in household appliances.

Hairdryer

Blow

The electric motor in a hairdryer turns a fan to blow air that is heated by hot wire coils. A switch adjusts the speed of the motor. The larger the current it allows through, the stronger the magnets become, and the faster the motor spins.

Suck

A vacuum cleaner has a powerful electric motor that turns an air pump. The pump sucks air through the machine, where the dust is removed from it. The motor has to generate a lot of power, so it needs electricity from the mains to drive it.

Vacuum cleaner

Turn

Many kitchen gadgets, such as food processors, have an electric motor that moves their working parts. Gears slow the speed of the motor, so the parts turn slowly. The electricity comes either from the mains or from batteries.

Food processor

James Watt

British engineer James Watt (1736–1819) improved the design of steam engines, and produced the first effective one in 1765. In 1774, he and Matthew Boulton began building steam engines for pumping water from mines. The unit of power, the watt, is named after him.

Timeline

1st century AD Hero of Alexandria, a Greek inventor, makes a novelty toy that is turned by steam.

1698 Englishman Thomas Savery (c.1650–1715) builds the first machine to provide power by using steam.

1815 British engineer George Stephenson (1781–1848) builds the first steam-powered locomotive.

Gears

1876 In Germany, Nikolaus Otto (1832–91) develops the first four-stroke petrol engine. It is a great commercial success.

1892 The diesel engine, used for driving machines, is patented by German engineer Rudolph Diesel.

1894 The *Turbinia*, the first ship with a steam-turbine engine rather than a piston engine, is demonstrated in England.

1937 The first jet engine is demonstrated by the British jet-power pioneer Frank Whittle (b. 1907).

FIND OUT MORE
AIRCRAFT | CARS AND TRUCKS | ELECTRICITY | FORCE AND MOTION | INDUSTRIAL REVOLUTION

ETRUSCANS

A PIRATE PEOPLE OF MYSTERIOUS ORIGIN, the Etruscans dominated the Mediterranean world from the 8th to the 4th centuries BC and formed a league of 12 city-states in what is now modern Tuscany, Italy. Though many of these cities – possibly the first in the area – have been lost over the centuries, superb painting and statuary remain. Etruscan fortunes, based on trade and conquest, started to decline after c.500 BC when the Romans, who had lived under Etruscan rule for a century, began to absorb their former masters into their own expanding empire.

Expansion
From their base in Etruria, the Etruscans' influence spread between the northern Alps and Naples. From 616 BC, the Tarquins, an Etruscan dynasty, ruled Rome itself.

Art

Vivid wall paintings have survived in tombs at the ancient cities of Orvieto, Veii, and Tarquinia – some dating to c.600 BC. Scenes often show dancing, religious observances, or the underworld. Etruscan art was influenced by the Greeks in subject matter and style, but as the Etruscan civilization grew it developed its own bold, colourful, and naturalistic style.

Offerings to the gods

Tomb frescoes often pictured dancing to honour the dead.

Musician

Wall painting, Tomb of the Leopard, Tarquinia

Cities of the dead
Rich Etruscans were buried in underground tombs, some of which were carved from the rock to resemble rooms. These cities of the dead contained frescoes, furniture, and lavish ornaments that tell us much about daily life.

Etruscan rock-cut tombs, Sovana

Bronze sculpture
The best sculptures were made in metal, especially bronze. Early sculptors made copies of imported Syrian or Phoenician objects, but then Greek styles became more popular.

Pan, the liveliest Greek god, in Etruscan style

Statuary
Etruscan craftworkers made statues of terracotta – a brownish-red, unglazed, fine pottery. The sculptors were particularly skilled at creating realistic human faces and figures, such as those at the precinct of Apollo in the city-state of Veii.

Etruscans adopted the letters of the Greek alphabet.

Bronze coin

Language
Though examples of Etruscan writing survive on coins and tablets, the language remains a mystery. All scholars know is that it was the last survivor of those languages spoken before Indo-European (from which all modern European languages descend) took over. The first six numbers were *mach, zal, thu, huth, ci, sa,* but no one can be certain which of them match the numbers 1, 2, 3, 4, 5, 6.

Pirates and traders

For centuries Etruscan ships dominated the area of the Mediterranean called the Tyrrhenian Sea. Feared at first as pirates, they later turned to legitimate and prosperous trade with the Phoenicians, Greeks, and Egyptians. This continued until they were eclipsed by Rome.

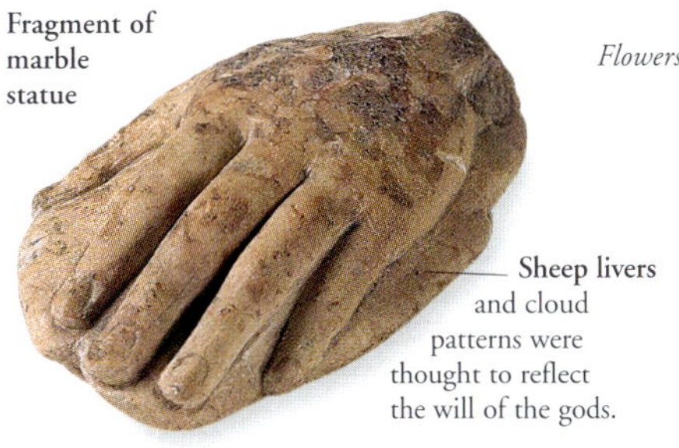

Fragment of marble statue

Sheep livers and cloud patterns were thought to reflect the will of the gods.

Relationship with Rome
The last Etruscan king was overthrown in 510 BC, as Rome took over the Etruscan cities one by one. Many practices, such as predicting the future by studying sheep entrails, lived on in the new Roman republic. Leading Roman families were proud of their Etruscan ancestry.

Trade
Etruscan agriculture, industry, and commerce all flourished in the period before the rise of Rome. Mineral deposits in the area were a great advantage to the Etruscans. Wealthy merchants traded metal products, such as jewellery and bronze figurines, as far away as Scandinavia and England.

Flowers

Naturalistic human features

Fruit

Gold earrings

Etruscan jewellers were especially good goldsmiths, and surviving pieces show originality and artistry. Much gold jewellery was made for trade with Greece.

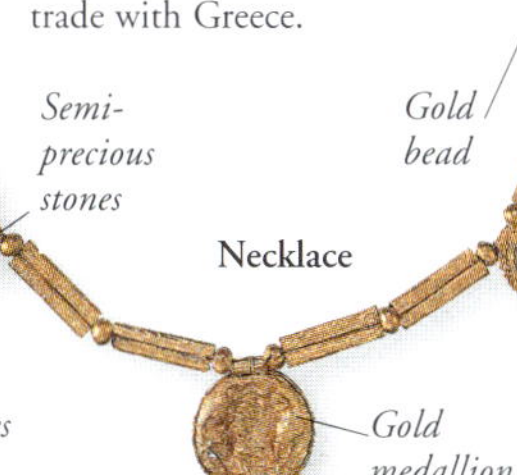

Semi-precious stones

Gold bead

Necklace

Gold medallion

Gold wreath hair ornament

City people
No one can be sure exactly which 12 walled cities formed the original Etruscan league. Ancient walls still surround today's Tuscan hill-towns, such as Orvieto. The original cities were built haphazardly, and each was dominated by temples.

FIND OUT MORE

ARCHITECTURE · ART, HISTORY OF · GREECE, ANCIENT · ITALY, HISTORY OF · METALS · RELIGIONS · ROMAN EMPIRE · SCULPTURE

EUROPE

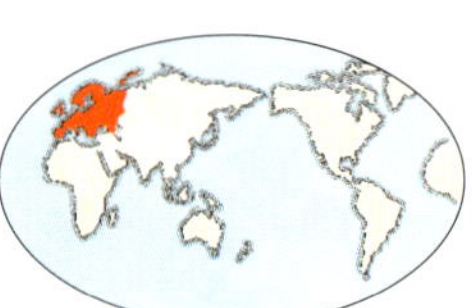

THE SECOND SMALLEST of all the continents, Europe nevertheless has the third largest population after Asia and Africa. Rich, fertile soils, a variable but hospitable climate, and abundant natural resources have made it easy for people to live in Europe for thousands of years, establishing more than 40 nations and much wealth. Shifting land borders and inhabitants of wide ethnic diversity have caused conflict, but Europe is politically stable and is a major world power.

Physical features

Europe's landscapes range from frozen tundra and coniferous forests in the north to the balmy Mediterranean coast and arid semi-desert of central Spain. The high mountains of the Pyrenees, Alps, Carpathians, and Urals give way to the low-lying North European Plain. Rivers provide communication and transport.

Ural Mountains
The Ural Mountains in Russia separate Europe from Asia. They stretch 2,400 km (1,500 miles) from the Arctic Ocean to the Caspian Sea. The highest mountain is Narodnaya at 1,894 m (6,214 ft).

North European Plain
The vast, rolling North European Plain extends from southern England, across France and Germany, and into Russia as far as the Urals. Rich in coal, oil, natural gas, and fertile farmland, this is Europe's most densely populated area.

Alps
The high Alps dominate western Europe. Stretching 1,500 km (932 miles) from southern France, through Switzerland, Germany, Italy, Austria, and Southeast Europe, this vast arc of mountains separates northern Europe from the warmer south. The highest point is Mont Blanc in France at 4,808 m (15,774 ft).

Cross-section through Europe

Fertile farmland on France's Atlantic coast rises to the plateau of the Massif Central and the Alps at more than 4,000 m (13,125 ft) above sea-level. It then drops down to the Hungarian plain before climbing upwards again to the Carpathians and down into the Black Sea.

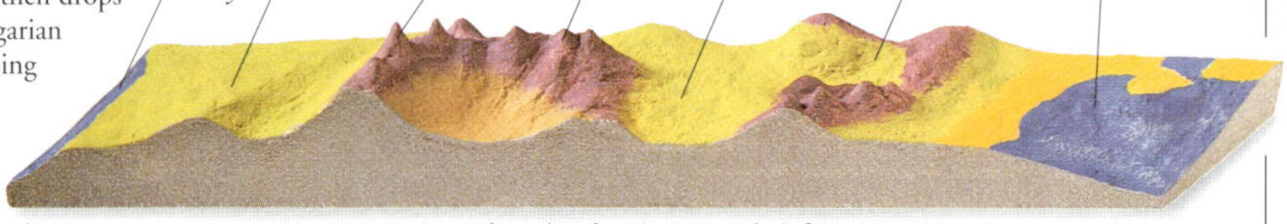

Approximately 2,400 km (1,500 miles) from A to B

EUROPE FACTS

AREA 10,400,000 sq km (4,000,000 sq miles)

POPULATION 704,900,000

NUMBER OF COUNTRIES 43

BIGGEST COUNTRY Russian Federation

SMALLEST COUNTRY Vatican City

HIGHEST POINT Mt. El'brus 5,633 m (18,481 ft), Caucasus Mountains

LOWEST POINT Volga Delta 28 m (92 ft) below sea-level, Caspian Sea

LONGEST RIVER Volga

BIGGEST FRESHWATER LAKE Lake Ladoga

Climatic zones

Europe's position and varied landscape greatly affect its climate. Apart from the far north where it is always cold, European winters are generally cool, and summers warm or hot. Europe's west coast is milder because of the Gulf Stream, which brings warm waters northwards. Mountains, such as the Alps and Pyrenees, form a natural barrier, protecting the south from the rain and cold winds that blow from the north.

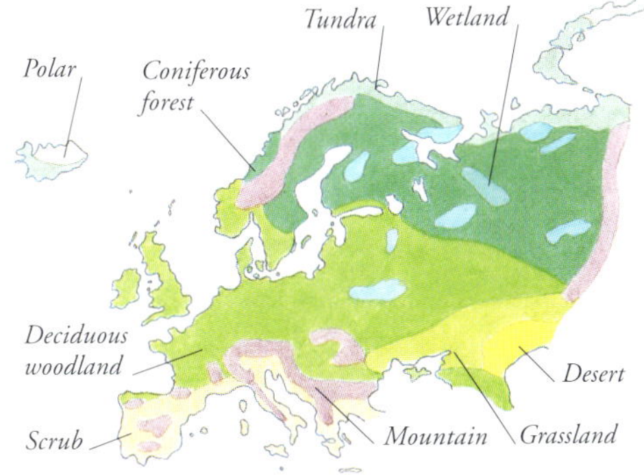

Only shallow-rooted plants can survive the cold.

Tundra

The extreme north of Europe lies inside the Arctic Circle and has a polar climate. The vegetation there is tundra – treeless plains where much of the subsoil is permanently frozen ground called permafrost. Only in summer does the topsoil thaw and plants flourish.

Deciduous woodland

Broad-leaved woods and forests are found in many parts of Europe. The trees, which lose their leaves in winter, include the quick-growing birch and ash, and the slower-growing, longer-lived beech, chestnut, maple, plane, and oak. Today, few ancient wild forests survive, and most forest trees have been planted.

Oak leaves and acorns

Beech trees lose their dead leaves in spring when the new buds sprout.

Straight trunks provide timber for making paper, furniture, and boards.

Taiga

In Russian, the word taiga means a marshy forest. The trees in the forests of northern Europe are mainly conifers, such as fir, larch, and pine. They keep their needle-like leaves even during the cold winters when they may be covered with snow for many months.

Pine-needles and cone

Grasslands

Large areas of Europe, such as the central *meseta* region of Spain and the steppes of southern Russia and southeastern Ukraine, are covered in vast expanses of grassland. Much of this land is used for grazing animals and growing crops. Drought can be a problem in extreme summer temperatures.

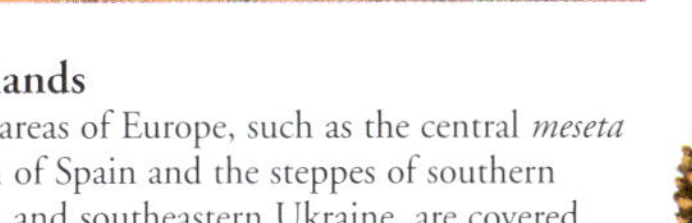

During the spring the grass is lush and green, but becomes scorched as summer progresses.

Many plants have small leathery leaves so they can conserve water in the summer heat.

Garrigue

The warm dry hillsides close to the Mediterranean Sea in countries such as Spain, Greece, and France are covered with thorny, often aromatic plants and low bushes. On limestone soils this vegetation is called *garrigue*, elsewhere it is *maquis*.

Ice, rain, and wind make it impossible for plants to survive on the peaks.

Pyrenees

The Pyrenees form part of a vast arc of comparatively young mountains that stretch almost continuously across southern Europe and join with the Himalayas in Asia. Unlike the ancient mountains in Britain and Scandinavia, their shape is still changing because of plate movements beneath the Earth's crust. Mount Aneto is the highest peak at 3,404 m (12,962 ft).

People

Most Europeans live in densely populated towns and cities, many of which lie on the fertile North European Plain. Living standards are generally high compared with other parts of the world, and Europeans benefit from plentiful food and good healthcare. Many countries have sizeable ethnic minorities, usually from former colonies. The majority of Europeans are Christian.

Finnish girl Greek boy French girl

Resources

Europe is rich in natural resources. More than half the land is used for farming a wide variety of food crops, from cereals, such as wheat, barley, and oats, to grapes, olives, citrus fruits, and salad vegetables. Europe mines 40 per cent of the world's coal and around 33 per cent of its iron ore. There are also large reserves of oil and natural gas, and lead, zinc, and other metals. Many rivers supply hydroelectric power.

Grapes

Wheat

Coal

CLIMATE CONTINENTS EUROPE, HISTORY OF EUROPEAN WILDLIFE FARMING FORESTS MOUNTAINS AND VALLEYS ROCKS AND MINERALS TREES TUNDRA

EUROPE, HISTORY OF

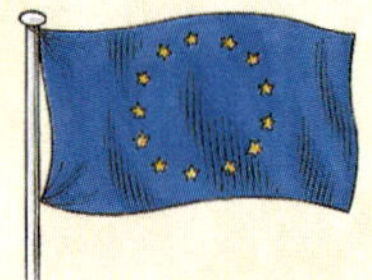

EUROPE HAS PLAYED a much more important role in world history than its small population or size would suggest. The Greeks and Romans colonized large parts of North Africa and western Asia, and from the 15th century onwards, European nations established trading empires that spanned the globe. The Industrial Revolution of the 18th century gave Europe an economic strength which allowed it to dominate world trade, and both World Wars began in Europe. Since 1945, Europe's global influence has declined, as wealth and military power has shifted to North America and Asia.

Prehistoric "Venus" figurine from Lespugue, France

Prehistoric Europe

The first settlers in Europe were primitive hunters who moved around in search of food. By about 5000 BC, people learned to farm and settled in villages. Bronze-working, and later iron-working, spread across the continent.

Civilizations of Europe

After 900 BC, four civilizations made their successive mark on Europe. The first were the Greeks, who created powerful city states. They were followed a century later by the Etruscans in Italy. By 200 BC the Celts had settled across Europe. Finally the vast and powerful Roman Empire spanned the continent, reaching its height in AD 117.

Ionic-style capital from ancient Greek temple

Greek Europe

The independent city states of ancient Greece got most of their wealth from trade. Their merchants sailed around the Mediterranean, and founded colonies from Spain to the Black Sea. The most powerful Greek cities were Athens and Sparta.

Latin inscription from a Roman tomb

Roman Europe

From its foundation in c.753 BC, the city of Rome gradually expanded its power until, by the first century AD, it controlled most of Europe. The Romans gave Europe a network of roads, a common language (Latin), and a legal system, all of which survived long after the fall of the empire in the 5th century.

Christian Europe

In the 4th century, Christianity became the official religion of the Roman empire, and over the next 700 years the faith spread throughout Europe. With the break-up of the Roman empire by 476 and the lack of any strong political force after then, Christianity became the single unifying force across the continent and the church gained great power.

Papal ring

Papacy

As head of the Roman Catholic Church, the popes had enormous spiritual power. Vast landholdings also gave the popes much political power, which led to many conflicts between the papacy and the leading rulers of Europe.

Orthodox icon of the Archangel Gabriel

East and west

Attempts by the pope in Rome to establish his jurisdiction over the entire Christian Church were resisted by the Orthodox Churches of eastern Europe, centred around the ancient city of Constantinople. In 1054, this schism (split) became final, leading to a religious division in Christian Europe that survives to this day.

College built around a central quadrangle

Merton College, one of Oxford's earliest colleges

Growth of education

The Church dominated education, at first through the monasteries and then the universities. The first university in Europe, specializing in medicine, was established at Salerno in southern Italy in the 9th century; others, such as Bologna, Paris, and Oxford, followed later.

The royal coat of arms of Philip II of Spain decorates the cover of one of his books.

Nation state

By the 16th century, centralized national governments had emerged right across Europe, from Spain in the west to Russia in the east. The Holy Roman Empire had began to break up, and in countries such as England power was concentrated in the hands of the monarch who ruled with the support of a parliament, composed of members of the aristocracy and church.

Henry IV of France was raised Protestant, but later converted to Catholicism.

Religious wars

The creation of new, Protestant Churches in the 16th century divided western Europe. Roman Catholic and Protestant states fought for supremacy in a series of bitter wars which lasted until the middle of the next century.

Basilica in Goa, India

Overseas empires

In the 15th century, European nations built up empires. Spain and Portugal colonized Central and South America; Britain, France, and the Netherlands colonized North America and the Far East.

World imperialism

The Industrial Revolution began in Britain in the mid-1700s, and it transformed world politics and economics. Within a century, European nations were strong and rich enough to set up colonies all around the world. Only the United States of America was able to resist European influence.

Diamonds

Hemp

Cotton

Global economy

During the 19th century, European steamships took raw materials from their colonies to factories in Europe, and shipped out finished goods to markets abroad. The huge industrial cities of Europe gained vast wealth, but at the expense of poor producers in African and Asian colonies.

Nationalism

During the 19th century, many of the peoples of Europe struggled to obtain their freedom from outside rulers. In one year, 1848, Italians, Germans, Hungarians, Poles, Irish, and others fought for independence or fairer forms of government.

Fighting at Catánia, Italy, 1848

Scottish private's cap

Austrian officer's hat

Soldiers' hats, 1914

World wars

Twice in the 20th century, European conflicts led to war on every continent. In 1914, national rivalries resulted in a four-year war that cost 22 million lives. Germany was defeated and dissatisfied with the peace treaty. Again, war broke out in 1939. By the end of that war, in 1945, Europe was exhausted. Two superpowers, the USA and the Soviet Union, now dominated international affairs.

End of empires

World War I led to the defeat of four great European empires – Germany, Austro-Hungary, Russia, and Turkey – and weakened both Britain and France. After World War II, Europe's overseas colonies fought successfully for independence, with only France retaining sizeable overseas possessions.

The double-headed eagle symbol of Germany

Flag of Nazi Germany

Rival ideologies

Communism was established in Russia after 1917 and in Eastern Europe after 1945, while Fascism and Nazism took hold in Italy, Germany, and Spain in the years up to 1945. By 1990, parliamentary democracy, at first weak in Europe, was the dominant form of government.

Iron Curtain

After World War II, Russian troops occupied much of Eastern Europe. A clear border, known as the Iron Curtain, emerged between the Russian-dominated east and American-dominated west. The border split Germany into two countries.

Checkpoint between two sectors of the city of Berlin

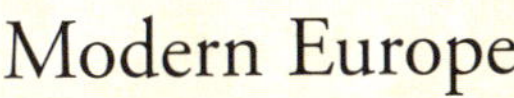

Modern Europe

After World War II, French and German politicians worked together to overcome their old hostilities. Economic collaboration between the two countries developed into a formal European Union that grew to include many other western European countries. With the collapse of communism and the rise of market economies in Eastern Europe, many former communist countries lined up to join the EU.

Collapse of Communism

During the late 1980s, Russia withdrew its military and economic support from its communist allies in Eastern Europe. Popular protests then overthrew communism in every East European nation by 1990, but by the late 1990s, there was deep unrest in many East European countries.

Revolution on the streets of Romania

Willy Brandt

Willy Brandt (1913–92) was born in Lübeck, Germany, but lived in Norway during World War II, where he was active in the Resistance. As Chancellor of West Germany from 1969–74, Brandt worked to improve east-west relations and made treaties with Poland and the USSR. He was awarded the 1971 Nobel Peace Prize.

Timeline

c.1250 BC Mycenaean culture flourishes in Greece.

c.900 BC Greek city-states gain power.

c.753 BC Rome is founded.

c.200 BC Celts spread across Europe.

Bronze statue of Roman legionary

AD 117 Roman Empire is at its height.

1054 Christian Church splits into Orthodox east and Roman Catholic west.

1500s European nations use their navigation skills to explore and colonize large parts of the globe.

Mid-1700s Industrial Revolution begins to transform the European economy.

1871 The map of Europe is transformed as Germany and Italy become unified nations.

1914–18 World War I.

1939–45 World War II.

Flag of European Union

1940s–80s Europe gives up most of its colonies.

1957 EEC is set up.

1989–91 Communism falls.

1994 Outbreak of war in Southeast Europe.

2001 Euro is launched.

FIND OUT MORE

CELTS · COLD WAR · EMPIRES · GOVERNMENTS AND POLITICS · GREECE, ANCIENT · HOLY ROMAN EMPIRE · MEDIEVAL EUROPE · ROMAN EMPIRE · WORLD WAR I · WORLD WAR II

EUROPE, CENTRAL

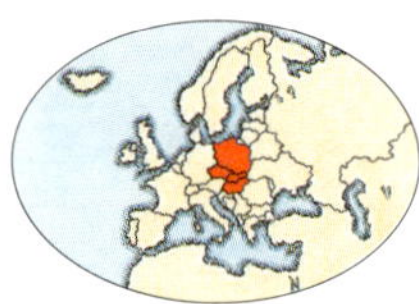

LYING AT THE HEART of Europe on the North European Plain, central Europe consists of four countries: Poland, the Czech Republic, Slovakia, and Hungary. With poor defenses because of the flat terrain, this historically troubled region has often been invaded by neighbouring powers and its country borders redrawn. At one time or another, French, Germans, and Russians have all dominated the area. After World War II (1939–45), the countries of central Europe became communist states closely tied to the former Soviet Union. Since their independence in the late 1980s, many have struggled to compete on the world market.

Roman Catholicism

In spite of repeated invasions of the area, and half a century of anti-religious communist rule, Roman Catholicism remains the dominant religion of central Europe. Throughout the region, colourful processions celebrate saints' days and other religious festivals.

Religious procession, Kraków, Poland

Physical features

Most of central Europe lies on the vast North European Plain and is largely flat, rolling farmland, broken by the low Sudeten and Carpathian Mountains in the south. In the north, rivers flow into the Baltic; in the south, they flow into the Danube on its way to the Black Sea.

Tatra Mountains
The Tatra Mountains between Poland and Slovakia are the highest part of the Carpathian Range. Their breathtaking scenery makes them popular with walkers in summer, and in winter the snow-covered peaks attract skiers.

Forests
Poland's Bialowieza National Park is the largest area of woodland in northern Europe. Some woods have survived for thousands of years, but acid rain now threatens them. One quarter of central Europe is forested.

Danube River
The Danube is 1,775 miles (2,857 km) long and links Germany and the Rhine River to the Black Sea. It is Europe's greatest waterway and is used for carrying freight and generating hydroelectric power in Slovakia.

Regional climate
Central Europe has a temperate climate with hot summers and cold winters. Winters tend to be milder in the south, except in the Carpathian Mountains and other upland areas where heavy snow falls. The summer months are often the wettest.

20°C (68°F)
-2°C (13°F)
553 mm (22 in)